A Career Worth Planning

Starting Out and Moving Ahead in the Planning Profession

A
Career Worth
Planning

*Starting Out and Moving
Ahead in the Planning
Profession*

Warren W. Jones and Natalie Macris

PLANNERS PRESS
AMERICAN PLANNING ASSOCIATION

Chicago, Illinois
Washington, D.C.

Contents

Acknowledgments

This book could and would not have been written without the late Albert Solnit, my co-conspirator and co-author of *What Do I Do Next? A Manual For People Just Entering Government Service*, published by the American Planning Association in 1980. Parts of the current book are derived from ideas that he and I developed in workshops and seminars conducted in the 1970s and 1980s.

I want to acknowledge others, too: one-time graduate students in the Departments of City and Regional Planning and of Architecture at the Berkeley campus of the University of California who were eager for a break from heavy-duty theoretical planning and design in favor of a connection with the "real world," which I represented as an adjunct faculty member from the world of private planning consultants. Also, pre-professionals who attended university- and APA-sponsored workshops in preparation for launching their careers. And unnamed local citizens and politicians with whom I worked as a private planning consultant during my entire career.

My special thanks to Natalie Macris, co-author, for joining me in preparing this document and for bringing a younger generation's perspective to bear on the continuing puzzles: what are we doing and why, for whom are we doing it, how do we prepare ourselves to do it well, and where and how do each of us fit in and gain satisfaction from practicing our craft?

Finally, several special people deserve mention for contributing their specialized knowledge, insights, and support: seasoned planner Daniel P. Farber; soon-to-be-college-graduate-en route-to-a-professional-life Noah Chalfin; Mayor Leslie Dahlhoff of Point Arena, California; and long-time community development director Wayne G. Goldberg.

Warren Jones

My first thanks go to Warren Jones, for inviting me to join him in writing this book. As his former student, I have long respected and admired his integrity and his understanding of planning issues, and especially career matters. The courses he taught at the University of California at Berkeley were a graduate school highlight for many students and provided a valuable introduction to the "real-world" tasks and responsibilities of being a city planner.

I am also especially grateful to the family and friends who helped with this book: Dean Macris, Marjorie Macris, Eric Macris, Ruthe Macris, Dean Palos, Jane Bassett, Leslie Katz, and Brian Thompson.

Many thanks also to the friends and colleagues—public sector planners, consultants, and nonprofit representatives—who contributed invaluable stories and observations through interviews: Drummond Buckley, Donald Dean, Deborah Holley, Sandra Meyer, Larry Orman, and Ceil Scandone.

Kaye Bock of the Department of City and Regional Planning at the University of California at Berkeley helped us a great deal by arranging an e-mail survey of students and recent alumni. Thanks also to the many students and alumni who responded.

The following people were very responsive to requests for information that helped round out our thoughts on career paths for planners: David Laverny-Rafter, Professor and Director, Urban and Regional Studies Institute, Minnesota State University, and Sharon Rue, Director, Career Advising and Placement, School of Architecture, University of Texas at Austin.

Finally, we owe many thanks to Sylvia Lewis, our editor at the American Planning Association, for her wisdom, suggestions, and patience.

Natalie Macris

Introduction

If you were going to visit a country you'd never been to before, you could just hop on an airplane, not quite knowing what to expect once you arrived in that unfamiliar place. But you would probably enjoy your trip more and get more out of it if you did some research and planning beforehand. You might consult guidebooks and maps, plan at least some of your time, and learn a little about the language and culture of the place you'd be visiting.

Beginning your career—especially in a field as broad and complex as the planning profession—is like starting any other kind of journey. You probably don't know quite what to expect. And you will probably find the trip more satisfying and enjoyable if you have read a bit about where you are going—and if you have some sort of game plan for yourself and for the situations you might confront.

This book is for you, the traveler to this new place. You may be graduating from a collegiate school of planning, or transferring into a planning job from a related professional job or professional school, or already in your first or second year of professional practice. No doubt you are or soon will be well grounded in the subject matter associated with the job you take. Presumably that is why you were or will be hired. In fact, if you are just emerging from a school of planning, public policy, environmental management, or public administration, your mind is probably full of numbers and means for manipulating them, with theories, propositions, and historical perspectives, with visions about what could or should be, and with some research and policy-recommending experiences and predilections. And yet, you may not have spent much time, or possibly any time at all, thinking about the practical skills you have to offer or preparing for your first year in a new professional-level job. You probably have not thought much about what employers are seeking from the available job candidates. You probably have given even less thought to the longer term, to building a career that you will enjoy and be proud of.

This book attempts to describe the principles and requisites for entering into the fray, whatever it may be for you, and for preparing yourself for some of the realities and challenges certain to face you in the early years of your career. It is about the characteristics and demands of work environments, and the aptitudes and skills you will need to perform well, survive, and advance. We focus on the concerns of employers, on the roles and behavior of politicians and citizens, and on the political machinations you will encounter in the offices and in the communities you enter. We provide practical advice for landing your new position, for surviving, adjusting, and learning on the job, and for building your career.

We intend this book to be a guide for men and women of any age who are entering employment as professionals or pre-professionals in any setting where planning takes place. While this book is chiefly directed to people entering, or thinking of entering, the field of urban (city and regional) planning or environmental planning, much of the information we provide may easily apply to other employment situations. You may be working for a municipal, county, regional, special district, state, or federal agency (i.e., not for a planning agency per se). Or, you may be employed by a nonprofit public health, housing, economic or community development, park and recreation, open space, land trust, or other advocacy or self-help organization. Other possibilities include being on the staff of a law firm or a real estate or housing development enterprise, or a member of a consulting firm, or an employee of a company or organization that seeks something from government agencies or interacts with them on a regular basis. Wherever it is that you work, you may be responsible for carrying out any number of tasks: research and data analysis, policy- and plan-making, permit processing, environmental analysis, data collection and management, urban or project design, advocacy, policy or plan implementation, transportation delivery, and so on.

No matter where you work or what your responsibilities may be, fundamental skills, knowledge, and aptitudes will be required. We attempt to set these forth in direct and unambiguous language. Our objective is to encourage you to think about what you need to do to meet work place needs, employer expectations, and your own professional development goals, and then to take action.

If you find that we are overwhelming you with too much reality, just keep in mind that our intent is not to scare you away from pursuing or continuing a career in planning, but to map out all or most of what will come along as you grow into your career. If you are about to enter employment as a professional for the first time, or are preparing to do so, Part I (Starting Your Career) may be all that you will want to tackle at first reading. If you are currently a planning professional with a year or two of experience who is trying to make sense of your work environment and your prospects for the future, Part II (Developing Your Career) is likely to be of most use to you.

At the very outset we advance a basic truth: What you learn and experience in your first two to seven years on the job will create the building block for the rest of your career. That's not to say that what you currently like doing, or think you most want to do, will inevitably resemble what you will be doing two or seven years from now, or at mid-career. In fact, it is impossible to expect that, at this moment, you can or should know exactly who you will be, what possibilities will exist, what skills you will have acquired, and in what setting you will practice them that far into the future. Nonetheless, the beginning years will allow you to find out about yourself and to explore the field of possibilities. You will master some skills, gain insights about work environments and the planning scene, develop confidence, and decide what tasks and settings do and do not appeal to you. These experiences will set the stage for your future career decisions.

Another basic truth: It has become very clear of late that, in industrialized or post-industrialized high-tech societies, continuing education and self-improvement courses and experiences pay off. Indifference, or a failure to grasp new opportunities and challenges or to keep alert to new technology and intellectual advancements, places one at a severe disadvantage when competing in the national and international employment marketplaces.

In short, even though your formal education may be over, there are still many things to learn, many trails to follow, and unlimited opportunities that you can only uncover and appreciate over time. With that in mind, we urge you to spend the next few years gaining some depth of experience and developing a full array of skills, remembering that one good thing leads to another. We strive to make this book relevant no matter what you may now think your goals are and no matter where you are headed next.

Part

I

Starting Your Career

1

The Planning Profession and You

The planner's universe is expanding. Historically, the public sector has been the domain of planners, and their traditional focus has been land use and urban design. Increasingly, though, planners are finding work—and a growing range of work—in the private sector and in nonprofit organizations. And they are finding opportunities to plan for much more than the optimum use of land and the built environment. Technological advances, meanwhile, are changing the nature of the workplace and the direction of many careers. People starting out in the planning field have opportunities that did not exist a generation ago.

WHERE DO PLANNERS WORK?

The generalist nature of a planning education can make planners suitable for many different kinds of jobs. The term "planning" itself refers as much as anything to an *approach* to problem-solving and goal achievement. The "planning" profession can thus be all-inclusive. Many planners can move into all sorts of situations where the approach they take to things is a marketable talent—a talent not necessarily shared by co-workers who have come out of other disciplines and whose focus may be comparatively narrow, highly specialized, and not comprehensive in scope.

Defining the "Planner's Approach"

The talents and skills that a planner brings to a job usually add up to a unique approach to solving problems and achieving goals. That approach typically involves the following:

- Seeing how facts and technical information relate or do not relate to the "bigger picture";

- Identifying gaps in needed information, expertise, and resources;

- Finding solutions by serving as interpreter, intermediary, facilitator, orchestrator, and negotiator among parties that are at odds or do not understand each other (between highway engineers and citizens, for example);

- Establishing a linear process for achieving goals: who needs to do what, and by when;

- Knowing how to make mid-course corrections;

- Knowing how to "package" findings and recommendations for public consumption; and

- Knowing how to get things done.

It sounds simple—so simple that it's hard to imagine that the planner's approach is unique, or even unusual. Nonetheless, the most important tasks that planners carry out—regardless of where they work—usually involve some form of this basic approach. And many planners find that the specialists they work with—architects, engineers, geologists, biologists, attorneys, and many others—are (rightly) immersed in their own disciplines and often unable to carry out the functions described above. That's what makes the planner valuable.

Typically, your first job (and usually most jobs after that) will require certain basic skills: researching, organizing information, writing, speaking clearly (in meetings, sometimes in presentations before fellow professionals, the public, or elected officials), interpreting policies and regulations, and making recommenda-tions (see Chapter 2, "What Employers Are Looking For"). Your first challenge in looking for a job is to choose the arena in which you can apply those skills most effectively, knowing your own particular strengths, abilities, interests, and personality. The three arenas where planners most often find work are the following.

The Public Sector

The public sector consists of governmental and semi-govern-mental agencies that are funded with taxes and other public money. These include city and county planning departments; re-gional, state, and federal agencies; and special districts (which plan for and regulate utilities, solid wastes, parks and open space, public transit, transportation, housing, and other services). Such agencies can range in size from just a few people to several hundred. In a small agency—the planning department of a small town, for example—an entry-level person might have a variety of duties, from working at the zoning counter to helping prepare the town's General Plan. In larger agencies, duties and roles are likely to be more narrowly defined.

The Private Sector

The private sector is made up of privately owned entities, such as consulting firms (land use planning, civil or geologic engineer-ing, economic and market analysis, architectural, environmental analysis), real estate development companies, law firms, and other businesses. The size of these offices and the nature of the work they do vary even more than in the public sector. Some con-sultants work individually out of their homes; others work for companies with staffs numbering in the hundreds. Some con-sulting firms provide one specialized service, like GIS mapping; others offer a whole range of services—site planning, environ-mental review, and general plan preparation, for example. Pri-vate-sector offices also vary according to the geographic area they cover. Some consulting firms and real estate developers only work locally or regionally; others have projects across the coun-try or throughout the world. Consulting firms also differ accord-ing to the clients they serve, with some firms working mainly for public agencies, some for other consulting firms, some for real es-tate developers—or all of the above.

The Nonprofit Sector

The nonprofit sector consists of organizations typically established for a specific "do-good" purpose and funded by endowments, foundation and government grants, and donations. Nonprofit groups differ according to their mission, geographic scope, and general style. One group might focus on research, developing methods of preserving agricultural land at the national level, for example; others might take on a more politically active advocacy role, seeking economic development in a single neighborhood, or open space retention and management within a region. Staff size and general solvency might also vary. These organizations are usually governed by a board of directors made up of influential citizens, sometimes self-selected and often elected by a membership of which they are a part.

What Planners Do

Here are some shorthand words and phrases commonly used in the profession that quickly identify what planners do. (They even may come in handy at parties when, inevitably, you're asked, "What do you do?") Sooner or later you might latch on to one or more of these as your way of telling yourself and others what you do as a planner. As time passes these words will take on depths of meaning based on months and years of experience practicing the art and craft of planning in one context or another. So, we might think of the planner as:

Facilitator	Project manager
Educator	Designer
Evaluator	Idea person
Editor	Analyst
Chief communicator	Enforcer
Monitor	Galvanizer of action
Agency or firm conscience	Number cruncher
Guerrilla in the bureaucracy	Nuisance
Coordinator	

WHAT ARE THE DIFFERENCES?

The basic skills required of you will probably be similar in whatever sector you choose, especially in your first job. Of course, different jobs will emphasize different skills; at a consulting firm, you might spend most of your day researching and writing, while at a real estate development office you will probably spend more time working with project plans and spreadsheets. Some of these skills you will learn by doing. At the outset, it may be more useful for you to consider some potential differences in the day-to-day work life of public, private, and nonprofit employees. This may be an opportunity for some soul-searching, in which you think about questions ranging from the profound ("Who am I and what am I good at?") to the mundane ("How much does having a regular lunch break every day matter to me?"). Again, you may not want to obsess over any of these distinctions in the beginning. There's a lot to be said for experimenting early in your career by trying out different job experiences and discovering what works and doesn't work for you. Nonetheless, planners often gravitate to one sector or another because of distinctions like the following.

Advocating the Public Position

Whether they are interpreting a zoning regulation or preparing a comprehensive plan, planners who work for government agencies often need to determine what would be in the best interests of "the public." This can be a challenging assignment, when "the public" is made up of many different (and often opposing) constituencies. Private-sector people may also confront the "public interest" question—when they're hired by a public agency to design a park or prepare a citywide plan, for example. In many cases, though, private-sector work—preparing a technical report, advocating a real estate development project, and so on—is less directly concerned with a broad "public interest." (The exception is when the consultant's client is a public agency and the consultant is acting as a substitute for agency staff.) Nonprofits, too, may be working on behalf of important public goals—affordable housing or open space protection, for example—but usually these goals are quite specific and aimed at a particular constituency, rather than at the "general public." That's not to say that, if you take a private-sector or nonprofit job, you won't care about the greater good—just that defining the "public interest" may not be the central question you will consider in your work.

Playing Politics

*Starting out in
your career, you
may find it advan-
tageous to have
close contact with
the political machi-
nations that affect
so much of what we
do.*

Because elected officials are ultimately responsible for most planning decisions, politics will be a factor in your work, regardless
of which sector you're in. But politics usually play the greatest
role in the work life of public-sector employees, who often serve
as staff to elected or appointed officials. Many consultants, real
estate and housing developers, and nonprofit advocates also
work in a political arena, and need to learn how to do so effectively because what they want to accomplish depends on their
ability to convince elected officials of the merits of their ideas.

Starting out in your career, you may find it advantageous to have
close contact with the political machinations that affect so much
of what we do. And you may find that you enjoy politics. If not,
you might consider a job that casts you in a slightly different role.
Specialized types of consulting such as historic preservation,
computer-generated mapping, or air quality analysis may provide opportunities for staying in the planning field but farther
away from the political arena, at least early in your career. (Later
on, you might be called in as an "expert" to help resolve political
disputes—or to help start them.) Technical support jobs at state
and federal agencies may also offer similar distance from politics.

Seeing the Results of Your Work

This can be an important advantage of working in the public sector: having an opportunity to see how your work plays itself out
in the "real world." When you are a planner for a city government and are working on a neighborhood plan, for example, you
may later be able to help carry it out. You may be put in charge
of handling development applications for the neighborhood, or
designing the new trail system called for by the plan. This gives
you a valuable chance to see what worked about the plan and
what didn't.

By contrast, the private consultant your city hired to prepare the
environmental impact report on the neighborhood plan may not
have the same opportunity to watch what happens after the plan
is approved. Similarly, the staff person from the nonprofit housing group that helped shape the plan probably won't have the
same day-to-day experience with carrying it out, since the nonprofit probably won't be responsible for executing or administer-
ing the plan. On the other hand, people who work for some types
of nonprofit or private organizations often do see the results of

their work, when an affordable housing project they developed or a park they planned is built, for example. Nonprofits, too, can often point to a long list of related accomplishments that give them satisfaction and suggest real progress in reaching their goals.

Knowing Lots of Jurisdictions, or Just One

In the private sector, you may have the chance to learn about many different jurisdictions. The consulting firm or real estate development company you work for may have projects in lots of different cities in your area, or across the country, or internationally. And the characteristics of the projects and clients will vary substantially from one to another. If you work in local government, you will get to know your jurisdiction very well, but may only occasionally have the chance to find out what others are doing. Those opportunities may only come along if you're asked to attend a conference or take on a special research project. In the nonprofit world, the geographical scope of your work will vary according to the type of organization you work for; some nonprofits are focused on one city or neighborhood, while others work regionally, nationally, or internationally.

Having Contact with the Public

In local government, you will often have more direct, ongoing contact with your constituency—the people who are affected by the work you do. This can have its ups and downs. If you are a planner who lives in a small town and also works for the town government, you may not relish the idea of having people come up to you in the supermarket to tell you what they think about the proposed new shopping mall. On the other hand, having closer contact with the public can have its rewards. One planner working for a planning department in a small city tells of handling a use permit application for a day care center, a good project that the Planning Commission had inexplicably denied in the past. This time, the application went smoothly, the Planning Commission was pleased to approve the project, and the day care operators were delighted. Several months later, during the holiday season, the planner received in the mail a Christmas card containing a "thank you" note and 20 colorful thumbprints from the day care children.

ZONING COUNTER

This sort of thing rarely happens to a private consultant who sails into town, submits a report, and then immediately goes on to another project in the next town. (Consultants who have lengthy and comprehensive contracts with local agencies, however, are likely to have extensive contact with the public.) Direct contact with the public is also less common at some (but not all) non-profit organizations that are more research-oriented and less directed toward on-the-ground results. Many planners with regional, state, or federal agencies also have far less contact with their constituents than local government planners do. For some planners, that is a blessing; for others, it is a missing element.

Networking vs. Regulating

In the private sector, you will often find yourself asking people for things you want or need. You may be calling government agencies to request information, networking with other consultants to drum up work, or marketing your firm in an interview for a new project. Certainly you will be persuading and selling others on an idea, a project, or a recommendation. Similarly, if you work for a nonprofit group, you will probably find yourself gathering information from various sources, forming alliances with other groups, or selling your organization or project to achieve a political goal or win a grant.

In contrast, as a public-sector employee, you will probably find that much of your day-to-day work involves people who come to you wanting things (zoning advice, a permit, a public works or consulting job contract); you will be in the position of "regulator," deciding what you can give out and what you can't. This distinction is not universally true; some public-sector planners deal exclusively with policy- or plan-making, duties that are less strictly regulatory and more proactive in nature. But often the most important (and sometimes troublesome) task of a government employee may be to say "no"—to recommend denial or the wholesale redesign of a badly conceived development application, for example. Or to work with others to achieve common goals even if compromises are required to do so. Or to explain the rules and regulations and to find ways, through persuasion or education or leverage, to cause others to comply. By contrast, private-sector and nonprofit people may have less occasion to say "no"—but they may hear it more often (when their bid for a new project or a grant isn't successful, for example).

Often the most important (and sometimes troublesome) task of a government employee may be to say "no."

This may not be a critical distinction in your first job. Still, it's worth thinking about whether you're someone who will be more comfortable "regulating" (i.e., giving out things and sometimes withholding them, or "policing" what others do, or engaging in various forms of negotiation in order to achieve desired outcomes), or "networking" (i.e., asking for things and sometimes not getting them, or engaging in cooperative ventures of one kind or another). While some people perform equally well in both roles, many prefer one over the other—or intricate combinations of elements of each.

Keeping Track of Your Time

In a private-sector or nonprofit job, you will probably be required to keep track of the number of hours you spend each day on each project you're working on. This allows your office to monitor your time and make sure that the total budget for each project is not exceeded. In the consulting world, hours spent on a project that a client is paying for are called "billable hours," while time spent on other, administrative tasks (reading your mail, for example) is "non-billable." Consulting offices will want you to minimize non-billable hours, and it may take a fair amount of self-discipline to do so, especially if you transfer from public to private work.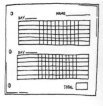

Unlike private-sector workers, government employees don't usually need to keep a precise record of how much time they spent doing what. (In fact, the "time-is-money" concept that governs the private sector may be foreign to them.) Some government agencies have introduced the idea of keeping an accurate record of employees' time project-by-project; cost recovery programs (i.e., charging applicants for the full cost of processing development applications) are one example. These records typically don't have the serious financial or accountability implications that they can in the private sector, however.

Knowing Your Work Schedule

In a public-sector job your hours will usually be fairly predictable. Your daily work hours will usually be fixed, and you typically won't have to work overtime without notice. You may be asked to attend public meetings at night, but again these will usually be scheduled in advance. (For some, however, there may be many such meetings, since a great deal of the public's business is accomplished at meetings scheduled late in the day or in the evenings when the public is most able to attend.)

In the private or nonprofit sector, your work life will probably be a bit less routine. Your boss may ask you at the last minute to put in some long hours on a crash project, and then let you make up for it with some time off later. In a private-sector office, particularly, the pace is generally driven by project deadlines; this means that you may have a period of furious activity, followed by days, weeks, or even months with relatively little work. During the slow times, you may be able to take longer lunch hours or make an impromptu office field trip to a baseball game—flexibility that the public sector doesn't usually offer. (Keep in mind, though, that if you advance to a management position this flexibility will probably vanish.)

Getting Paid

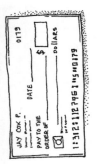

Salaries will vary according to many factors: the type of work involved, skills required, geographic location, and the local, national, or even international economy. Generally speaking, public-sector jobs are secure, pay reasonably well, and offer good benefits. Private-sector work can also sometimes (but not always) pay well, although salaries tend to fluctuate more and benefits may be less attractive compared with public-sector positions. Nonprofit jobs typically aren't quite as secure and don't pay as well as other types of work, but can offer more intangible benefits to people drawn to the advocacy role of these organizations.

WHERE TO WORK FIRST?

O pinions differ on which sector provides the most valuable experience for your first job. If you hold a private-sector or nonprofit job first and then move to the public sector, you may offer your government employer some fresh ideas on how other jurisdictions are doing things. You may also have a good sense of how to manage your own time, which you learned from your experience with project budgets and (in the case of private-sector consulting) billable hours. On the other hand, you may have to adjust to a new role as a government regulator who represents official policies to the public, and who determines and advocates a "public position." If you previously worked as a nonprofit housing advocate or a real estate developer, for example, you may find that making a recommendation on a housing project is more complicated when you are a public-sector planner. Who will benefit? Will anyone be harmed? If so, do the advantages still outweigh the disadvantages?

If you hold a public-sector job first, you will have the advantage of knowing how government agencies operate. This can be very useful if you then move to a nonprofit or private-sector job, particularly if those government agencies become your clients; your recommendations to them will be based in reality and reflect your knowledge of how things are actually done. On the other hand, you may have to become accustomed to keeping track of your time and monitoring project budgets. You may also have to become familiar with networking and marketing your firm or organization to potential clients or benefactors. For example, job interviews—which you may have previously experienced only as an unpleasant necessity for landing your own job—will be something you face constantly when you work for a private consulting firm that bids on projects in different cities or with many different clients.

An important consideration: It is not uncommon for private-sector employers to avoid hiring someone whose sole, and perhaps too lengthy, work experience has been with a public agency. The standard bias is that public employees are not familiar with the concept of "time is money," have learned "bad habits" (such as ambivalence and laziness) while working in a bureaucracy, and cannot be expected to have developed the drive, adaptability, and attitudes of a professional working in a profit-making enterprise. A real estate developer, in particular, may suspect that a job candidate from the public sector does not have enough entrepreneurial spirit to fit the bill.

Conversely, public agency employers are sometimes suspicious that long-time private-sector or nonprofit people will not know how to represent a truly "public" position or handle themselves properly and with patience in public hearings. And both public- and private-sector employers may worry that a nonprofit veteran will still be championing a cause in ways that will interfere with his or her performance in a different type of job (one that emphasizes housing data analysis rather than affordable housing advocacy, for example). Whether these biases are just or not, they are worth keeping in mind as you explore and develop your career goals.

TYPICAL CAREER PATHS—ARE THERE ANY?

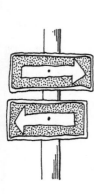

A re there typical career paths for planners? The answer seems to be the proverbial "yes and no." Some people gravitate toward government work and stay there for the duration of their careers because they appreciate the relative job security and the sense of working for a "public good," or because they simply are not attracted to private-sector venues. Others enjoy the pace and the demands of private consulting, or the entrepreneurial aspects of real estate or housing development. Still others thrive in the more activist environment of nonprofit organizations. These inclinations often reflect basic personality traits and job skills that help determine the course of a career. For that reason, it is not unusual to find that career paths gravitate toward one sector or another early on, and stay there.

On the other hand, many people find it healthy and energizing to change course at some point in their careers. Early on, especially, you can learn by experimenting, say with an internship at a local planning department or nonprofit group, followed by a year or two of work for a private consulting firm. It's also increasingly common for people with 10, 20, or more years of experience to make big changes, as a way of gaining a new perspective and avoiding burnout. Some successfully make the transition from public to private or nonprofit sectors, or vice-versa (perhaps confronting and overcoming some of the biases described above). Some move into a different type of job within the same sector, by becoming a city manager after serving as a planning director, for example. Others go further afield, to become division chiefs at state or federal agencies, executive directors of nonprofit groups, housing agency chiefs, public health officers, practicing attorneys, university researchers or faculty, state legislators, city council members, or planning commissioners with an attitude. Still others start their own businesses—either by becoming independent contractors or by forming new firms—after working for others. And still others find it beneficial to take a break from planning altogether—to take a sabbatical or a year off for traveling, or to start a totally unrelated business.

As they proceed through their careers, many planners discover opportunities that they didn't know existed. Often these opportunities occur serendipitously, and may be invented along the way in response to some need or funding availability that no one today could predict. If you have an entrepreneurial streak, staying alert to and mentally prepared for such opportunities can help you make of them what you want. Also, keep in mind that as time goes on you have more and more to offer, sometimes even skills you do not at this reading know you are capable of mastering.

When you are first starting out, you will probably have no idea how your career is going to unfold. It's important to remember that either approach—the steady building of a career in one sector or technical expertise, or the accumulation of job experiences in many different ones—can be perfectly acceptable and very productive. The point is to figure out what works best for you.

Either approach—the steady building of a career in one sector or expertise, or the accumulation of job experiences in many different ones—can be perfectly acceptable and very productive.

FINDING THE RIGHT ENVIRONMENT FOR YOU

The first step to finding the right work environment is to jump in somewhere, begin to develop your skills, and learn what you truly enjoy and are good at. In doing so, keep in mind that the experience each person has on the first real job is not unlike the experience everyone your senior already has had. The new employee is uncertain and often insecure. The ways of the workplace do not resemble the ways of academia, and day-to-day operations, community politics, office politics, professionalism, ethical issues, and career planning are not usually part of the college curriculum.

In short, few of us are totally equipped for our first job. We usually begin with a set of "generalist skills" and perhaps some essential and useful specialist skills. Some of us already know we would be most comfortable in a technician's role, while others want to be more active, perhaps even political, and maybe even become top managers. But we are shy on experience, mere beginners in developing social-personal, communication, and management skills. And we rarely know anything about office politics, the essential culture of organizations, or the reasons why things are done the way they are, which at times are contrary to our expectations, values, or ethical standards. These skills must be learned on the job—but often there is little time to learn. This book seeks to expedite the on-the-job learning process, and to encourage the kind of self-evaluation that leads to productivity and growth.

Some Career Paths

To illustrate some typical career paths, here are brief descriptions of some planners we know and the routes they have chosen or happened upon. An important point to notice: None of these people charted out every detail from the beginning, and some not even the general outlines of a complete career path. (Names and a few details have been changed to protect the privacy of these friends, acquaintances, and colleagues.)

Louis studied political science as an undergraduate in the early 1950s, and got excited about city planning after visiting European capitals during a stint with the U.S. Army. He enrolled in a city planning graduate program (which was then in its infancy), and started work at a large city planning department. After working his way up in the ranks, he migrated cross-country, becoming assistant director and eventually director of planning for another large city, a post he held for many years. He retired from the public sector in the early 1990s, and since then has served as a consultant on a variety of high-profile planning and development projects in the western U.S.

Lee studied landscape architecture and park planning in college, where she also took a few introductory city planning courses. After working for a short time for an architecture office, and later a housing developer, she found that she was more interested in public policy than in real estate development. She took an entry-level job at the planning department of a medium-sized town, and worked several years there before moving on to a more senior planning position in a larger town. She has worked with that planning department for 10 years, mainly on current planning projects (i.e., development applications), and has been promoted several times. She has recently negotiated a work schedule with her employer that allows her more time to be with her children.

Fred, as a high school student, thought he might like to become an architect. He got interested in city planning in college, where he took courses in urban design and the history of the built environment. He earned a master's degree in city planning in the late 1980s, and worked in the planning departments of several medium-sized cities. After several years of public sector work, he moved to the private sector, working for a small consulting firm preparing environmental impact reports. After about two years there, he decided that he preferred local agency planning work and the public contact that comes with it. He took a job at the planning department of a small suburb, where he is managing the processing of a large, complex, and controversial development application.

Sharon began her career managing commercial real estate investments for a large bank. She became interested in the process by which development decisions are made, and concerned about environmental degradation associated with real estate speculation. These concerns led her to take planning courses, and eventually to earn an undergraduate degree in urban planning. While still in school, she accepted an internship at a regional government agency. After she graduated, she applied for and received a permanent position as a regional planner at that agency. In her 10 years there, she has managed projects ranging from subregional planning programs to campaigns promoting government and public awareness of regional air and water quality issues.

Greg earned a master's degree in urban and environmental planning in the 1970s. Immediately after graduating, he took a job with a nonprofit organization that promoted open space preservation and growth management in a large metropolitan area. He moved up the ranks in the organization, eventually becoming its director, a position he held for almost 20 years. He resigned in the mid-1990s and formed a new nonprofit group that provides computer mapping services and environmental information to other nonprofits.

He also teaches courses in open space planning and regional growth management at the planning school where he earned his degree.

Robin started out as an architecture student and an apprentice architectural aide in the mid-1950s, and like others at the time found architecture intellectually limiting given his interests in large-scale project design and the workings and design of cities. His completion of a graduate program in city planning served as a partial solution to that dilemma, and led to his becoming a small-town planning director. He then turned to freelance consulting work, followed by employment with a "new towns" planning and architectural firm in Scandinavia. (At that time, comprehensive new town developments were commonplace throughout western Europe, and opportunities for planners with architectural training and skills were abundant.) He spent the balance of his career as a professor of planning in a major Southwest university. After retirement from teaching, Rob was employed part-time by the Federal Emergency Management Agency (FEMA) and now practices what he preached—he is a determined, well-informed, and skilled citizen activist in a suburban city in the Pacific Northwest.

Andrea earned a master's degree in journalism and planning in the 1950s, and wanted to become a newspaper reporter covering urban affairs. Finding that job opportunities with newspapers were limited for women in those days, she took a job as a planner for a large city. After more than 10 years there, she migrated to the West Coast, where she held progressively responsible positions at a county planning department and eventually became its director. She moved on to become planning director for a medium-sized city before retiring from the public sector in the early 1990s. Since that time, she has worked as an interim planning director for various cities in her area, and as a consultant and project manager for local agencies processing large development applications. She also volunteers her leadership and policy analysis skills to nonprofit groups involved in local planning issues.

Hank received an architectural degree and practiced architecture for many years before returning to school for his master's degree in city planning. After working for a noted California planning consultant, mostly on the development of local comprehensive plans, he acted on his true interests and impulses and served for many years as a local elected official and mayor. In these capacities, he was well-equipped by virtue of his education and experience to steer planning and policy adoption toward the progressive goals he had long championed. Hank topped off his political career as a state assemblyman and co-sponsor in the California legislature of ground-breaking legislation designed to manage and protect the California coastal zone.

Dave started his career in the 1960s as an undergraduate in a Midwest city planning program, after which he entered a West Coast graduate program and earned a city and regional planning master's degree while working part-time at a nearby consulting firm. He then elected to stay on to earn a Ph.D., one of the first in city planning. For the next two decades he held top positions as economist and policy analyst in an internationally known research and development company. He is now CEO and president of an eminent public policy research institute that is funded with money from the foundation arm of a global computer hardware giant.

Jim received his city planning graduate degree in the mid-1960s and then practiced in a consulting firm before entering employment as a mid-level bureaucrat in a state agency. From that point on, his career was as assistant director of a state planning and research agency, followed by executive director of another state agency, and then executive director of the Sierra Club, a nationwide citizen activist and educational enterprise. After many years in that role, and still being only at mid-career and obviously destined for management roles, he returned to public employment as executive director of still another state planning and land management agency. While he spent very little time doing any traditional planning or plan-making—his calling was to take on challenging top management roles—his work consistently involved directing others to prepare plans and to advance the causes and goals of the agencies and nonprofits of which he was a part.

Doug always knew he wanted to be a planner. His first job after graduate school was as the second-in-command in a two-person rural planning agency, where he did "a little of everything" with no time left over to tackle real plan-making. The next step was taking on the planning directorship of a small town, followed by several years as an independent consultant. As family needs required a steady and stable salary plus benefits, he applied for and landed a job as a park planner responsible for development of land use and resource management plans for newly acquired large-scale parklands under the jurisdiction of a state park and recreation agency. This job requires advanced technical skills (data management, mapping, resource identification, user surveys), plus the ability to assess future user needs, coordinate the input of other professionals, specialists, and the public, write faultless analytical and policy reports, and lay out land use and resource management plans suitable for consideration and action by the state's legislature and governor.

Eve learned about the planning field while completing an undergraduate degree in social ecology in the early 1980s. While still in college, she served as a planning intern at the community development department of a medium-sized California city, where she worked on projects in both current and advance planning. She went on to earn a master's degree in urban planning, and held internships in both the public and private sectors while still in graduate school. This on-the-job experience allowed her to work as a contract planner for a few months before obtaining her first full-time job at a medium-sized consulting firm that specialized in environmental review. After two years there, she moved to another similar firm, where she was assigned increasingly responsible project management duties. Three years later, she moved to another consulting firm to become a senior associate. After five years at that firm, she took a pregnancy leave, and returned to work part-time when her son was a year old. With the birth of her second child, she resigned her job to become a full-time mother. She attends planning conferences and may rejoin the workforce once both children are in school.

Cal was born, raised, and educated in California. He went to Canada for his graduate planning education and then returned to the United States to pursue his career goals. After the standard apprenticeships in various local planning agencies, he was hired by a planning consulting firm and gradually rose to become one of the partners. As satisfactory as his rise to senior status and authority was, he harbored a sense of uneasiness and took a lengthy leave of absence in Britain. As was true for many in the 1970s, the comparisons between British and North American planning policies and practices were striking, enlightening, and sometimes disturbing, and the results of planning efforts in California seemed unsatisfactory and well below his notion of what was possible. His sense of uneasiness upon returning to his firm translated into a realization that he didn't want to be a planner. The time in Britain allowed an idea to germinate, and the result was that Cal and his wife thought through and implemented a program to lead North Americans on instructional walking tours throughout Great Britain. These tours were for adults interested in historic places and their preservation, policies and techniques for preserving special landscapes, and post-war British town planning accomplishments, mixed with sight-seeing, visits to historic places, and predetermined long country walks. For some 20 years this has been his career, a blend of interests in and knowledge about planning and his interests in things British, coupled with an easygoing and mellow lifestyle free of those aspects of planning practice that he did not like, such as working long hours, attending evening meetings, balancing project budgets, managing staff, playing politics, writing reports, and dealing with quarrelsome politicians and demanding clients.

CHAPTER

2

What Employers Are Looking For

In this chapter we are largely concerned with the beginning of your career. To that end, we focus here on traits and skills that employers look for when seeking and selecting new employees to fill entry-level professional positions, positions that inevitably lead to more and more responsibility and the need to develop still more skills. Later in this book we address in detail all of the essential skills required for advancing your career and professional development goals.

What employers are looking for when selecting one person from among several available candidates depends on the character of the agency or firm, the expectations of the hiring employer, and the work to be done. While there are many traits and aptitudes that virtually every employer is looking for, not all of them are readily measurable—but that makes them no less important. Some will not apply in every employment situation, but are likely to apply some time in your career and are fundamental for a fully rounded and effective professional. As you prepare to enter a professional setting, you need to be aware of these basic traits and certain essential aptitudes, as well as those essential skills that all employers expect job candidates to possess or seem likely to be able to master over time.

Employers will consider your academic record and work experiences—but they will be looking for much more.

BASIC TRAITS AND APTITUDES

If you are just entering the work world, you may think that employers are most interested in your academic record and the working and life experiences you have accumulated so far. Employers will consider these, but they will also (and perhaps mainly) be looking for much more. The following traits and aptitudes are not necessarily listed in order of importance—all of them are important. Although you need not have mastered all of them when you are being considered for your first employment opportunity, bear in mind that employers hope you possess all of them. Employers will make allowances if you are an entry-level candidate, while insisting on them for more senior positions.

- Dependability and reliability, which include showing up on time and completing assigned tasks when expected or promised.

- Specific aptitudes and skills consistent with the responsibilities to be assumed and the tasks to be undertaken.

- A potential for growth leading toward assuming more and more responsibility.

- Ability to anticipate needs of your supervisor and even to take over when necessary.

- Diligence, focus, and self-discipline.

- Ethical standards.

- Absence of personal, ideological, and political agendas inconsistent with the position, assignment, situation, and mission of the agency or firm. (Even if your agendas are not actually inconsistent with the agency's or firm's, you must demonstrate the ability to keep them under control and not allow them to bias your work or your fair treatment of or relations with others.)

- Aptitude for becoming a skillful communicator by speaking and especially by writing clearly. (You may be "forgiven" for being unable to design or map, or for less than an optimum facility with numbers, but never for being unable to write well and with minimal supervision.)

- Being able to size up a work assignment, figure out what to do, prepare a work program, and get the assignment done on time—sometimes with very little guidance or help from others.

- Being truly able to listen to the client and to recognize that solutions and ways of doing things often do not emerge from the planning theories and principles you may have picked up here and there, but from the mouths of a mixed bag of people with whom and for whom you are working. (These same people may hold the right to question or reject your advice, employ delaying tactics, make mistakes, act foolishly, or make choices based largely or strictly on political considerations.)

"You can observe a lot just by watching."
—*Yogi Berra*

- Being able to proceed strategically and sometimes incrementally. (Sometimes a direct and straight line from A to Z, or a solidly laid-out comprehensive approach, may seem logical to you but cannot be readily accepted or implemented by your boss, your client, or others, nor understood and subscribed to by others, for whatever reasons. Nevertheless, your job will be to present the means for proceeding logically, systematically, and according to schedule, and often to take a leadership position yourself in order to make things happen.)

- Being able to explain to and educate your client about the findings you make and the policy ideas you favor. (You must be clear and explicit, able to present and defend the alternatives you are considering, and able to lay out the consequences or impacts of one choice or action over another in precise and simple terms—and sometimes with dollars attached. You must also be able to back off when it might be inappropriate or counter-productive to push too far or too fast.)

- Being able to "package" your findings and proposals. (Clients usually have relevant ideas and goals, often very well and sometimes passionately expressed orally. It is usually the case, however, that they do not have the time or know-how to write cogent and well-organized reports and plans, nor do they necessarily know how to proceed systematically through a long and often arduous process leading to problem resolution, policy adoption, or other action. Here is where planners typically have a great deal to offer, and you must be prepared and able to deliver.)

- Being able to empathize and understand the points of views and needs of others, especially those who are members of another profession, socioeconomic group, race, or political persuasion.

- Being aware that the art of effective planning often is the art of compromise.

These qualities and traits are fundamental, tailored to the planning profession but applicable elsewhere as well. Consider a recent survey among business executives who asserted that workers need "soft" skills even more than technical expertise. Fully 80 percent of this diverse group of senior executives ranked certain skills as "very important" in the following order:[1]

- Listening skills: 80 percent

- Interpersonal ("people") skills: 78 percent
- Problem-solving skills: 76 percent
- Technical writing skills: 71 percent
- Basic computer knowledge: 70 percent

Note that being able to hear what others are saying stands at the top of the list. We take this to mean not just listening but truly hearing and understanding what is said, and the meanings behind what is said, by bosses, fellow workers, board members, citizens, and political leaders, including those who may be saying things you find bizarre or discomforting.

ESSENTIAL SKILLS REQUIRED

"Always be smarter than the people who hire you."
—Lena Horne

No matter what the venue or who interviews you for an available position, your interviewers will also be judging you based on what they perceive to be your level of skill in the following categories. It is not that you will necessarily be judged negatively if you have not mastered each one of them. Rather, your interviewers will judge you based on whether or not you possess some of these skills (depending on the specific requirements of the available job), and also on whether you seem to have the potential for mastering the others as time goes on. Bear in mind, too, that not only are these the skills employers are looking for, but they are also the skills that you most assuredly will want to master for self-fulfillment as an accomplished and seasoned professional.

Generalist Skills

Generalist skills include the background needed to know why you are doing what you are doing and for whom. To some extent, generalist skills are learned on the job, and they are improved over time as one works in diverse settings with diverse people who contribute to the richness of one's outlook and perspective. The most effective generalists have academic or professional degrees, are liberally educated (meaning they know something about a full range of subjects from art to zoology, are reasonably well read and aware of current events, and have some rich life experiences), and are familiar with the literature and central ideas associated with the work they are doing and the society in which they are working and living.

Specialist Skills

Specialist skills are those needed to perform the specific tasks assigned and/or to match the job description of a particular position. Each function requires its own specialists. While managers may not be specialists in anything, they cannot function without a roster of people who are trained and experienced in the relevant specialty areas. Examples of planning-related specialties include computer mapping and simulation, historic preservation, general plan preparation, environmental analysis and review, current planning, traffic analysis and circulation design, and code enforcement. In each case, specialists are trained to carry out a well-defined technical or research task or service. Their effectiveness and value to the agency or firm depend primarily on professional education and training at the beginning of their careers, supplemented by continuing professional education, and on the accumulation of on-the-job experiences over time.

Research Skills

Anyone working at a professional or technical level must have the ability to generalize from available data and observation, and at the outset know what information is needed and what is not. If the data and information are not provided to you at all, or in an unsatisfactory fashion, you will need to know what to look for and how to get it. You must fully understand the nature of the problem you're trying to analyze and solve and have the ability to attack it in an intellectually creative fashion. Your attack may include literature and public record searches, surveys, listening to and recording information from interviews, and identifying problems, wants and needs. (See also New Technology Skills, below).

Social-Personal Skills ("People Skills")

To work effectively with others no matter what the setting, you must be able to (a) cope effectively with stress, (b) cope with difficult people, (c) foster interpersonal relations, (d) handle client services effectively and be responsive to client needs, and (e) contribute to an harmonious relationship with fellow workers and your supervisor.

Communication Skills

On the job, you must be able to perform most of the following as soon as possible: (a) write memos and reports in jargon-free, clear language; (b) draft, draw, and communicate graphically and with photography—even if in only rudimentary fashion; (c) speak before the client, fellow professionals, and the public; (d) participate in and facilitate meetings (as opposed to remaining mute when your input may be needed), and if necessary run a meeting; (e) give directions clearly when required to do so; and (f) be able to respond to requests from the media (unless your boss explicitly reserves that function to him or herself, which is often the case).

Work Programming, Budgeting, and Time-Management Skills

Regardless of whether or not you are seeking a management post, you must be able to understand and handle the following: (a) work programming, coordination, scheduling, and causing others to get things done on time; (b) time management—of yourself and those who report to you; (c) organizational planning and development, and office management; and (d) job or project monitoring. You also will need to show skills in (a) effective leadership and supervision; (b) employee development and the orienting of new people to the job and the agency or firm; (c) employee utilization and job satisfaction; (d) delegation of authority and responsibility; (e) budgeting and fiscal management; (f) conflict resolution through negotiating, brokering, and mediation; (g) communicating with others on behalf of your agency, firm, or client; (h) inspiring productivity and loyalty; and (i) working effectively with politicians.

Stylistic Skills

At the heart of the question of effectiveness are the stylistic skills of attitude, approaches to problem-solving and work itself, work habits, judgment, and ability to command respect. No matter how skilled as a generalist or specialist, no matter how well trained and seasoned as a manager, you cannot expect to lend support to, assist, or influence others, effect change, mediate differences, sell new ideas, facilitate the support of decision-makers, or please your client if you are surly, lazy, insensitive to the needs of others, arrogant or patronizing, or a poor listener or obsessive talker. Your style as an employee is crucial not only as it influences whether your job is done well, but as it affects your own capacity to grow and develop professionally. In short, your personal style needs watching just as much as your writing and your research skills do. If your style gets in the way of your effectiveness or relations with your client, you may be faced with a decision about what to do to change, or where else to find employment or your life's work.

New Technology Skills

Skills are needed to keep up with new methods or processes and to use new computer programs. In a fast-moving society and global economy, new ways are constantly discovered to record, process, and present information and ideas. Anyone who started working in the 1950s, for example, can tell you that it has become necessary to relearn almost entirely how to undertake and complete many standard tasks, especially those associated with managing data, mapping, and assembling and presenting findings in ways that lay people can readily understand. In the 21st century, your skills in these areas probably will need to evolve even more rapidly. Included may be knowing how to do research on the Internet, updating your agency's or company's web site (or parts of it that pertain to your work), and perhaps other things that no one can foresee and specify today.

Political Skills

It often comes as a surprise, especially to those who regard planning as a purely technical or artistic endeavor, when someone utters the mantra "planning is politics." While there are office politics, and inter-departmental or inter-agency politics, your greatest concern may be community politics, and how not to lose sight of the fact that planners often function in highly charged political settings among community leaders, politicians, elected officials, and citizen activists. Politics for planners is the art of functioning well in a setting where people vie for influence or votes and have power over outcomes. All who function in public and quasi-public settings have developed or are in the process of growing their own political skills, and surely will be obliged to exercise them as occasions demand. You need to be ready to do the same.

Advocacy and Lobbying Skills

Notwithstanding that most job descriptions are silent on the point, and that lobbying comes too close for comfort to real politics, it would be naive to assume that a professional planner's job ends at producing the perfect research report, plan, implementation program, or ordinance. The job also includes selling one's (or the agency's or client's) ideas among decision-makers and engaging in some form of (discreet) lobbying. Senior planners learn to accept this role as a skill worth mastering, and some do it much more skillfully than others.

TO SUM UP

Bear in mind that in a job interview you do not want to turn glassy-eyed when confronted with questions about your accomplishments and level of expertise in the above categories. The interviewer will not necessarily dismiss you as unworthy if you have not had vast experience in and a mastery over these skills, but he or she may do so if you display ignorance of or indifference to their ultimate importance and significance in the workplace.

The best jobs, and especially those requiring increasing responsibility, are in the hands of a few people who will check you out with a few other people by telephone or e-mail.

In addition to being judged on your basic traits and aptitudes, as well as on the demonstrated accomplishments you have in some of the categories of essential skills cited above, it is good to be aware that to be worth hiring and promoting, you must have something to offer. You are going to be hired for your skills and potential, not because of your degree or list of experiences, although both help establish your credentials or at least open the door to an interview. What's likely to be especially impressive is what you can do and what other people say you can do. (The best jobs, and especially those requiring increasing responsibility, are in the hands of a few people who will check you out with a few other people by telephone or e-mail.) The more skills you have in your kitbag, the better. And, the proof is in the pudding and not in what you allege in your resume. (See Chapter 3 for guidelines on resume writing and preparing for an interview.)

Another important thing to bear in mind is that employers have two basic objectives, in addition to wanting to hire the most skilled of the available candidates. They want (a) mature and competent employees, and (b) loyal and "safe" employees. There is no room for boat rocking, radical chic, disagreeable behavior, and unreasonable chance-taking. So, in addition to the marketable skills we are discussing here, you also need to think about (and maybe work on) your personal attributes and your stylistic and "people" skills.

Having familiarized you with the essentials, we now want to set forth what else truly impresses people who ultimately do the hiring. If you can convince these people that you have these qualities as well as the others just cited, you are likely to be among the top final candidates. The qualities that really count are:

- Demonstrated writing abilities, including the ability to produce reports on your own in finished form that are (virtually) flawless and always persuasive.

- Demonstrated ability to make presentations to others skillfully and with no obvious signs of fear, to field questions and challenges, and to remain poised and (mostly) unflappable even in the face of skeptical or possibly hostile challenges or confrontations.

- Demonstrated ability to take assignments or projects all the way through from beginning to end in a timely manner, and to be a self-starter who is able to work independently and yet is equipped emotionally to take direction and criticism.

- Demonstrated "people skills." These include being able to listen—even to those who may be cynical, hostile, egomaniacal, power-hungry, or otherwise not easily abided. They also include keeping your mouth shut lest you make things worse by being defensive (or offensive) or argumentative, and working hard to accommodate alternative points of view with which you may not be in agreement (but without seriously compromising your own principles).

- Demonstrated understanding of the culture of the venue (the firm or agency, or the firm's client or the community) and the way things are done.

Of course, as a new arrival into the marketplace, you may or may not yet possess all of these characteristics and it may take time to do so. They do indeed apply more to those who are en route to a position beyond their first entry-level job—but that does not make them any less worth pondering beginning on Day One of your job search, and later throughout the tenure of your first professional job. Surely they are germane when you are under consideration for subsequent and more senior job openings and promotions.

Finally, and notwithstanding that all of us expect to be judged and measured fairly and on the basis of strictly objective criteria, it is clear that employers are also looking at, scrutinizing, or double-checking with others the following:

- How appropriately you are dressed and groomed,

- Your overall demeanor,

- Your disposition,

- Your life experiences as clues to your general view of yourself and the world, especially if they may be related to what you can do or will be doing,

- Your level of maturity, and

- Your potential for fitting in among existing staff.

As one city planning director told us about having been faced, over a period of many years, with sorting out exactly whom to hire from among several often essentially equal and potentially very competent and well-credentialed candidates: "Everything counts—including hunches."

Notes

1. *Time* magazine, June 28, 1999.

CHAPTER

3

Landing Your First Job

Even if you have a good sense of yourself, the skills you have to offer, and where you might like to work, finding and getting a job—especially your first job—can be a complex and demanding process. Finding job openings, writing resumes and cover letters, interviewing, and networking can be a stressful business for even the most intrepid candidates. This chapter gives some tips to help you negotiate this maze.

THE JOB MARKET: MYTHS AND REALITIES

It may be worthwhile to consider at the outset some myths and realities about the job search process:

Myth: Your credentials will get you the job.

Reality: While they are certainly important, your credentials alone will not get you the job. Planning agencies and consulting firms stress skills, rather than credentials such as degrees, professional memberships, years of experience, and former job titles. This may be a reflection of unhappy experience with university graduates who weren't up to par, even though their academic records were impressive. Consider the employer's point of view. Would you choose solely on the basis of test scores, performance in school, and experience carefully presented in a resume? It is doubtful that you would, particularly if you had many candidates. You would probably choose someone who demonstrated a clear understanding of your needs and presented himself or herself as the sort of person who could meet those needs.

Planning agencies and consulting firms stress skills rather than credentials.

As a job applicant, you may be asked to describe the specific work, education, or training experiences that have enabled you to acquire a skill or knowledge. You may then be assessed on how well you will apply these attributes to situations that might arise on the job. The lessons are simple: Be sure you know what you claim to know, possess some recognizable skills, and can assure others that you can apply your knowledge to work situations.

Myth: It is possible to predict personnel needs.

Reality: No one can predict future needs accurately enough for individuals to plan careers based on current advice. It's best to rely on your interests—and your instincts—to guide you to where you want to be and to make yourself aware of the roles and opportunities that are or may be in demand in the near future.

Myth: Somewhere there is a system or institution that can reliably link the job hunter to the job.

Reality: What exists is imperfect, and does not always function fairly or in the best interests of the job hunter. For many civil service jobs, there are written tests and lists upon which applicants are placed and chosen for interviews, maybe months or even years later. For other jobs, it is only a matter of being interviewed on the basis of a job application and resume. And many well-paying and desirable jobs in the planning field are not advertised through normal channels at all; these jobs are filled by personal contacts or by chance.

Myth: A good resume will get you the job.

Reality: Resumes are definitely important, but mainly as a tool for getting you to the most important stage: the job interview, where you can talk persuasively and honestly to the person who has the power to hire you. You should make sure that your resume clearly, thoroughly, and honestly conveys that you have the qualifications needed for the job you are pursuing. But don't assume that your resume alone will get you the job. (For some civil service jobs, your resume matters not a whit, since you will be expected to fill out an established personnel form designed to supply information about you and your relevant past.)

With those realities in mind, here are some tips to prepare you for the job of finding a job.

FINDING JOB OPENINGS

The job-hunting process can take a long time, especially if you are new to the profession or if the economy is weak and jobs are scarce. It's best to try a wide variety of the following approaches. Cast your net widely; in particular, don't dismiss internships or other low-paying or volunteer job opportunities that would get you in the door of a place where you would really like to work. The result may be that you would be first in line (as a known commodity) for a proper job when one comes along.

Cast your net widely—don't dismiss internships or other low-paying or volunteer job opportunities that would get you in the door of a place where you would really like to work.

Publications

Newspaper want ads are one obvious source of job listings for the public and private sectors as well as nonprofit agencies. University and municipal reference libraries also typically carry other publications that advertise jobs in the public sector. In addition, almost every state has a publication put out by the state league of cities or municipal league. American Planning Association (APA) chapters and other professional organizations publish newsletters that often list public and private sector job opportunities.

Even if they don't contain job listings, newsletters and other publications might lead you to potential employers. For example, consulting firms often advertise in newsletters; you might check off a few that sound interesting, do more research, and contact them about future work. Even the local telephone book can be a source of information; look in the government listings (or in the Yellow Pages under the logical headings) for agencies, consulting firms, and nonprofit groups you might not have bumped into elsewhere.

Internet Listings

Most federal, state, and local government agencies maintain World Wide Web sites that contain job listings. Many consulting firms and other agencies also list job opportunities on their web sites. There are indeed examples of job hunters securing positions posted on the Internet, sometimes after trying all other avenues in vain.

Beyond job listings, web sites are a valuable source of background information about the agency or firm that might hire you. A consulting firm's web site, for example, might list projects recently completed by the firm, the background of the firm's principals, and other information that will be useful to you in interviews and other contacts with the firm.

The APA web site (*www.planning.org*) provides services for people interested in planning-related jobs. These include job listings, links to local APA chapter web sites (many of which also list job openings), links to other Internet job listing and career service sites, and lists of books and articles of interest to job seekers. The APA web site also contains an international database of consulting firms that might be useful if you are looking for a private sector job.

You can find a multitude of other career services on the web. Career service web sites might help you find specific job listings, track down information on a specific firm or type of firm, or lead you to agencies or organizations you didn't know about. These web sites might also provide more generalized information useful in your job search (tips for resumes, interviewing, etc.). Some web sites also provide resume matching and distribution services—you input your resume, and the site sends it out to recruiters and prospective employers. Guidebooks dealing specifically with Internet job search resources can help you navigate this maze. Be forewarned: You will probably spend a lot of time at your computer and find that planning-related jobs are not as well represented as jobs in other professions.

Employment Services

Your college or university may maintain listings of planning-related jobs. The college alumni association may be able to match you with a job or with an agency where you would like to work. The state or federal employment service office may also be a source of job leads.

Other local employment services (career counseling groups, for example) may be able to help with some aspects of your job search. Even if the people at these organizations don't know much about the planning field (which is often the case), they may offer a useful critique of your resume and suggestions for making job contacts.

Networking

Personal referrals can come from friends, professors, university placement officers, or other classmates who are already employed or actively looking. You might also make good contacts by attending conferences, business functions, lectures, and conferences and job fairs sponsored by your university or college or by planning organizations (like the American Planning Association or the National Association of Environmental Professionals and their local chapters).

Some of your contact people may agree to do "informational interviews" with you, even if they don't have a job to offer you at the moment. These interviews (in person or by phone or e-mail) give you a chance to learn more about the career directions that interest you, advertise your skills, and get referrals to others who might be hiring.

Don't forget to send thank-you notes to the people who have helped you.

The Direct Approach

This might also be called "pounding the pavement" or "going door to door," maybe preceded by phone calls or maybe not. This approach involves dropping off resumes at places you're interested in, and possibly lucking out and finding someone (maybe even the hiring staff member) in the office willing to talk to you. Rejection is more than possible—it is likely. But jobs have been secured this way; at least a follow-up interview is possible. This approach does require a somewhat assertive personality. What you will be banking on is being instantly liked and given special treatment on the spot. Timing may be everything! (Note: Don't bother trying this with public agencies, since they typically don't have the flexibility to hire people in this manner.)

A variation on this approach is to research an organization you think you would like to work for, identify a service you think it might need, and then contact the organization to see if you can make a "deal": "I will deliver X if you will let me do Y." This approach probably won't be effective with a public agency, but in the private-sector or nonprofit worlds it could establish your reputation as a "go-getter" who can take charge and who may not require endless supervision. And you could land your ideal job this way.

Serendipity

Jobs can just fall into one's lap. One planner landed a job as a consequence of walking through an airport after five months in Europe and running into an acquaintance who headed up a private consulting firm. Small talk revealed that the planner was looking for a job, while the acquaintance was looking for staff. An interview three days later produced a job offer.

Another landed a job as a consequence of merely dropping off a resume at a consulting firm and hoping for the best. The timing was perfect, because two weeks later one of the firm's principals, who had just executed a huge public contract, was searching through the file of resumes for a specialist in regional water resource planning—a specialty the young planner had begun developing in a summer internship and succeeded in portraying well in his resume. The fit was ideal, the young man was hired for the two-year duration of the contract, and he remained on staff for several years thereafter as a proven and valuable staff person doing other kinds of planning projects. These things do happen!

APPLYING FOR WORK

Let's assume you've located a lead that seems to offer you a chance to work at something you would like to do. Here's what you'll need to do next.

Weighing Your Chances

At the outset, consider as objectively as possible whether you offer the right skills and level of experience for the job you're interested in. Also consider whether the fit between you and your potential employer seems plausible.

Difficult as it is, you should also try to assess whether you might be wasting your time on one of those nefarious (usually public) agencies that rob job seekers of valuable time and effort by advertising a vacant position that the agency fully intends to fill using in-house personnel. (The agency may be required to advertise the job to show compliance with affirmative action or other regulations.) One clue suggesting that your chances are almost nil will be if the agency has set a very tight deadline that is almost impossible for outside applicants to meet.

With these potential pitfalls in mind, here are your likely next steps.

Filling Out Applications

The general idea of application forms is to see if you wash out on paper. Some hints from personnel people include:

1. *Follow directions carefully.* For example, when you are asked for a description of the duties and responsibilities of your last job, write or type them on the form. Do not print "See resume on file." For complex questions, look elsewhere on the form for permission to add supplemental sheets as necessary.

2. *Be honest but diplomatic.* When asked about reasons for leaving a previous job, for example, give as true an answer as possible without sounding like a complainer or a troublemaker. Often, personnel people will check with past employers or supervisors before giving you an interview. It doesn't help to bad-mouth a former employer, even though the criticism may be richly deserved.

3. *Don't state your salary requirements right off.* While most employers have a salary range in mind, and in some civil service situations may be obliged to offer what is set down in regulations or law, salaries and step levels are often negotiable after you've been offered the job. Even if the employer requests your salary requirements, it's usually impolitic and strategically suspect to state a demand before you know you're wanted.

4. *Don't attach your resume (or other items) unless asked.* Personnel departments in public agencies typically rely on written applications that ask questions about relevant experience and education. These people do not usually refer to or want resumes unless the department head asks for them. That's why it's best to follow the application directions scrupulously, and only attach a resume if you are specifically asked to do so. Don't assume that padding things with resumes, photos, or even cover letters will increase your chances. You may in fact be doing yourself damage if you convey the impression that you are impatient with filling out forms and can't follow directions (see item 1 above), or if you appear to be uncommonly in love with your resume.

Writing Resumes

The main purpose of resumes and cover letters is to get you an interview. Remember, employers award jobs to people, not to resumes. With that in mind, keep your resume short; optimum length is one to two pages. This will allow your potential employer (who may have received hundreds of resumes) to home in on your special skills for the job. (An employer's eyes almost always go first to the skills and experience sections of a resume.)

The main things to list are all the basic activities and skills you have acquired in recent employment. Be thorough; you can never be sure what they're looking for. For recent graduates, it helps to put your educational record first, especially if you have impressive accomplishments (awards, scholarships, grants, honors) but little employment experience. Don't bother listing the courses you've taken or your grade-point average, though; most employers will be far more interested in any internship you've had. Do list summer jobs; even a few months of work as a waiter or salesperson demonstrate that you have experience with showing up at an appointed time, working with other people, and dealing with the public.

The main purpose of resumes and cover letters is to get you an interview. Employers award jobs to people, not to resumes.

Be judicious about listing references. If you were to follow conventional wisdom, your resume would indicate that references are "available upon request." The theory is that references are a precious resource—these people are volunteering their time to do telephone interviews, write letters, and fill out forms on your behalf—and therefore should be hoarded until you're being seriously considered for the job. But there is an alternative argument in favor of listing references on your resume (or in your cover letter—see below): If potential employers see the name of someone they know, they will sit up and take notice. Employers making big personnel decisions are often flummoxed, and a recommendation from a known person in favor of a particular candidate can be and often is the deciding factor. After making a spontaneous phone call to that person and hearing a favorable report about you, the employer might move your resume to the top of the pile. (Conversely, if the employer hears a bad report, or only half-hearted enthusiasm, your resume will probably go directly into the recycling bin.) The resume-with-references approach works better when you are applying for private-sector jobs, rather than positions at large public agencies with civil service requirements and/or personnel departments that screen the resumes. At any rate, a smart candidate will recognize these possibilities and act accordingly. Always ask permission before using someone's name as a reference.

A few more resume "don'ts":

- Don't list previous salaries on a resume, because they could either make prospective employers reduce what they were going to offer or make them think you're too high-priced.

- Don't put career objectives on a resume. If you really believe that such things will help you sell yourself to a prospective employer, include them (in terms applicable to a specific job) in your cover letter (if any).

- Don't list hobbies. They are irrelevant and only clutter up a resume. If prospective employers are interested, they can ask more about you at an interview.

- Don't include photographs, since they are irrelevant, often regarded with some embarrassment, may be seen as indicators of excessive self-regard, and may inadvertently prejudice an employer unfavorably (albeit unwittingly).

- Don't jazz up your resume by binding it or somehow making it look "cute." Anything other than a conventional presentation will not make any difference, other than putting you at risk of appearing pretentious and a bit desperate.

More than one version of your resume may be helpful. For example, a resume for an academic or research position should stress training, publications and professional presentations, teaching research, and so on, while a resume for a government agency job (should one be requested) should emphasize practical skills and abilities. A resume directed at a private firm or non-profit group should somehow convey your understanding of the "time is money" concept, perhaps by highlighting your experience in the private sector or by indicating how you produced results in a public-sector or academic setting. If you are responding to a job ad, it might be a good idea to repeat some of the ad's buzzwords ("management experience," "computer skills," etc.) in your resume. Remember: The purpose of the resume is to get you invited to an interview. Stress the qualifications essential to the job at hand.

Carefully proofread your resume, and ask a sharp-eyed friend to look at it for you, too. Don't rely on your computer's spell-check program; you will need an actual human to help you catch grammatical problems and other oddities. You might be surprised how many potential employers will toss your resume if it contains even a minor error. They figure if you can't get something as important as a resume right, your attention to detail on the job may be lacking, too. Don't give an employer this all-too-easy reason to count you out.

Writing Cover Letters

In some instances, cover letters are even more important than the resume, because they give you a chance to state explicitly what you offer to the place where you'd like to work. This is especially true when you are applying to private firms and nonprofits. Public agencies are typically more interested in your written application, and usually don't want to be bothered by either a resume or a cover letter; in these cases, your cover letter may just look like padding, or will end up in the recycling bin. Try to be judicious about when to send a cover letter.

If you do include a letter, make it brisk, personable, and to-the-point. The letter should contain three or four short paragraphs describing how you heard about the agency and/or job, and highlighting the special qualifications you have that don't fit within the format of the resume. If possible, do a little homework on the agency and mention how you might fill a need that wasn't mentioned in the job ad (if that's what you're responding to).

This is the place to mention why you want to work for this particular place in this particular job, and what you can do for this employer. This will often come up in an interview, so make sure you have clearly thought it out. The cover letter is also a good place to call attention to an especially relevant work experience you've had, or a key reference person whom the agency might want to contact. Avoid sappy and inane expressions about the high regard you have for the company or how you've always wanted to work there, unless you have serious and explicit reasons for making these claims.

Preparing Writing Samples

Make copies of some of your best work to bring to interviews or to send to your interviewers afterward. Keep the samples short (three to five pages maximum) unless your interviewer wants to see a complete document. Do not submit these samples unless you are asked to do so, and do not include them along with job applications.

INTERVIEWING

The purpose of an interview is to allow the potential employer and employee to get to know each other. More specifically, the interview process helps to reveal to the employer things about you that you might not volunteer on your own, or that cannot come through in an application or resume. These might include intangible qualities such as your overall intelligence, common sense, independence, ability to get along with others, willingness to work hard, and sense of responsibility.

If you have reached the interview stage, you are considered qualified for the job.

If you have reached the interview stage, you are considered qualified for the job. The interview is not so much about reviewing your qualifications as it is about establishing your personal style and ability to interact with others. Your primary goal therefore should be to make a good first impression and maintain it through the interview. Keep in mind that just showing up is not enough. Rather, look at the interview as a sort of tryout similar in part to what the director of "Les Miserables" or "Rent" must have done to find the perfect fit for the cast.

Before the Interview

Before you go into an interview, you should do the following:

1. Know why you want the job. (See "Preparing for the Interview" below.)

2. Know what you can do for your employer.

3. Know how much you're going to cost the employer if hired, or how little you'll accept as a salary.

4. When you set up the interview time, ask how long the interview will be, how many people will be there, and what materials (writing samples, extra copies of resumes, etc.) you should bring with you.

5. Do your homework before the interview. Research the community you will be working in, the agency you will be working for, and the programs you will be overseeing. This can only help you ask good questions and have an intelligent conversation with your interviewers. If you can, drop by your potential place of employment and note the general tone, mood, style of dress, and so on. This will help you figure out what to expect and what to wear to the interview. In fact, if you fail to do any homework it could show up in your interview.

6. Select your most relevant writing or other work samples to bring to the interview. You need not necessarily give these to the interviewer to keep.

Preparing for the Interview

Before you go to an interview, consider your qualifications in relation to the job at hand. Then think out and even rehearse the responses you are going to give to questions such as the following. Questions like these may actually arise during an interview, although it's unlikely that you will be asked all of them in one sitting.

1. What are your long-term goals? What do you want to be doing five or 10 years from now?

2. Why do you want to work for us? Why should we hire you?

3. What are your greatest strengths? Weaknesses?

4. Why do you think you are ready to take on the responsibilities of this job?

5. How long have you remained at previous jobs? Have you received promotions?

6. What are you looking for in this job? How will this job fit into your long-term plans? Why are you looking to change jobs?

7. What contribution can you make to our objectives? What can you do for us that you think someone else may not be able to do? That is, in what ways are you unique?

8. What are the three most important accomplishments thus far in your career?

9. Do you work well under pressure?

10. What (other than working here) do you want to do with your life? What are your interests, hobbies, and so on?

11. Are you willing to work evenings and some weekends?

12. What are your skills?

13. What skills do you wish you had that you don't now have?

14. What are you going to do about increasing your skills?

15. What is your attitude about belonging to a professional society?

16. What experiences have you had in supervising others?

17. What other positions are you considering?

18. Did you enjoy your last job? If yes, why are you leaving? If not, why not?

19. Does your present employer know you are looking for another job?

20. What are your salary requirements? (You are free to dance around this one if by answering directly you place yourself at a disadvantage when negotiating a salary later in the process.)

21. What did you like best (or least) about your last employer?

22. Do you intend to carry on any outside work?

23. Have you ever been fired or refused a promotion?

24. Do you prefer working with others or working alone?

25. Are you active in outside groups or organizations?

26. How many hours per week do you think a person should spend on the job?

27. What do you think of attending meetings?

28. If someone called you a name at a public meeting, how would you handle the situation?

29. What is your attitude about the employer-employee relationship in arriving at decisions?

30. What is the most rewarding assignment you have ever completed? How did you go about completing it?

31. Are you innovative? Explain?

32. Are you competitive? Explain?

Remember, some of these questions might put you on the defensive. Others may not be readily answerable. Still others, such as #10 and #25, can be sidestepped if you think they are an invasion of your privacy. The interviewer may not care as much about the answer as how you respond. Are you cool, or do you panic? Employers want to be sure you are worth hiring. They don't want any surprises later, and a good interviewer can use many facts in arriving at the conclusion: Should I hire this person, or will I be sorry later if I do?

A Few More Questions to Expect

Many interview questions are meant not so much to gather facts as to get you to reveal yourself. To do this, "stress questions" like the following might be asked.

1. *Leading Questions.* "What do you think of the statement that planners (engineers, administrators, and so on), like doctors, like to play God?" What a question like this is trying to uncover is how you'd handle statements from opinionated people at a public hearing or in the office. Answer calmly, thoughtfully, and reasonably. Be aware that humor can backfire and come across as flip in a situation like this. (One planner blew an interview by replying to this question, "If it's God you've got an opening for, planners will assume the role cheaper than doctors.")

2. *Personal Attacks.* "You've done a lot of skipping around from major to major and job to job. Why should we believe you'll change this pattern if you get this job?" Watch out! The interviewer is trying to find out how you react when someone pushes a personal button. Will you flare up in anger and hostility, freeze into silence, get defensive, or try to talk your way out? Any one of these could be fatal.

   Stay cool. It's okay to disagree—but softly. For example, you might pause, think, and reply with something like, "Yes, I did move around a lot when I was a student, but I felt I needed to find diversity in training and experience. Now I'm more certain of what I can do and what I want, and this job seems to be a good fit for my abilities and work preferences." Avoid bad-mouthing current or former employers. "I learned everything I could there," or "I was ready to move on to new things and more responsibility" are better answers.

3. ***Questions for Which There Is No Answer.*** This is a trap laid for phonies and know-it-alls. It's okay to say you don't know the answer to such questions. In fact, it's the only reasonable answer. You might answer some questions assertively and with finesse. For example, the question might be: "If you become our Planner II, how would you do a public services element for our city in three months?" You could say: "I don't know right now, but if I were hired, I'd be able to come back with an answer on what would be feasible in a short time and how."

4. ***"Tell Us a Little About Yourself."*** This question is the most difficult test for many. It tests your poise, warmth, communication skills, imagination, judgment, and self-esteem. Be prepared with a response that tells the story of who you are, what you have accomplished, and what you would like to do next, all in the context of your career and the job at hand. Be sure to fit in some of your pluses: "I'm good at working alone without needing a lot of direction, but I can also work well in a team situation, where I often feel the most innovative." Finish, wait for questions, and then solicit them if you feel you haven't registered. Never just recite your resume. Your interviewers already have that; this is an occasion for you to add personal details, and to show how well you think and communicate without props.

Note: It is smart to bear in mind that the interviewer could very well be an imperfect person, as are all of us in one way or another, or has been assigned a role with which he or she is uncomfortable. That being the possible case, it is in your interest to "just be yourself," as authentic and genuine as possible under a trying situation, and not to second-guess what the interviewer seems to be looking for.

The "Real Life Situation" Interview

These types of interviews are increasingly common, especially in public agencies and usually for mid- or higher-level positions. Instead of asking the more standard interview questions, your interviewers will have you participate in an exercise designed to show how you would respond to a real-life job situation. For example, your interviewers might hand you an in-box full of items that need your attention, and ask how you would handle each one. Or, the interview panel might act as a Planning Commission,

"Real life situation" interviews test your understanding of the job responsibilities, your ability to set priorities, and your capacity for working under pressure.

and give you a short time to prepare and present a staff report. Or, your interviewers might pose a scenario in which the city manager bursts into your office saying that the mayor needs something, just minutes before you have to leave work to catch an airplane.

These scenarios test your understanding of the job responsibilities, your ability to set priorities, and your capacity for working under pressure. This type of interview can be difficult to prepare for; your performance will depend mainly on your common sense and your understanding of the job you're interviewing for. See if you can find out if the interview will be structured in this way, or if these types of questions are likely. Then spend a little time thinking about the day-to-day situations you might confront on the job, and how you might respond.

During the Interview

If you have solid answers to all of these questions and the scenarios that might come your way, you are now quite well prepared. Some tips on handling yourself during the interview:

1. Arrive on time (or a few minutes early), and be polite to everyone you encounter (not just the interviewer). Don't assume that the boss will not ask the secretary or receptionist what he or she thought of you.

2. If facing an interview committee, make a special effort to be loose, brief, and clear. Don't fill in silences with sales talk. Silence is golden to interviewers who have been looking at tense, eager strangers all day.

3. If offered a cup of coffee or a cold drink, take it. The time taken to get it for you slows down the process of getting started and, once delivered to you, it's a good prop and use of nervous hands.

4. Have paper and a writing instrument for taking notes. This indicates that you are serious about asking your own questions and recording the answers.

5. Pause to collect your thoughts before answering a difficult question, and ask for clarification if you don't understand the question. Keep your voice even and smooth and reply calmly. (And remember, it's okay to say "I don't know" sometimes.)

6. Be pleasant, make eye contact, and be aware of your body language.

7. Don't hesitate to ask questions about the job, and about company/agency policies, procedures, benefits, and so on. Save your best questions and comments for the person who counts—the person who has the power to hire you.

8. Don't be negative. Don't, for example, bad-mouth former employers. Your interviewers have no basis for knowing if you're right or not, and they may suspect that you just have a bad attitude.

9. Don't act cocky, flip, or overconfident. You may have many great qualities, but if you brag too much you may strike your interviewers as so inner-directed that you'd be difficult to direct from the outside. Avoid conveying the attitude that you are a hot-shot from a hot-shot school. Employers usually are not especially impressed with academic accomplishments, unless you are seeking an academic or technical research job.

10. If any of your reference people are likely to say something negative about you, try to anticipate it and explain the situation to your interviewer (again, as even-handedly and diplomatically as possible).

11. Don't accept a job on the spot (or reject one either). You will need time to "sleep on it," think about what you're getting into, and see if any more questions come to mind.

12. Before leaving, ask when you can expect to hear back from the interviewer. Invite him or her to contact you with follow-up questions, and thank everyone involved for their time and interest.

After the Interview

Promptly write a thank-you note that reiterates your interest in the job and your understanding of what will happen next ("I look forward to hearing from you next week," "I will call you next week," etc.). Use a business letter format; an e-mail is not advised, nor is a Hallmark card.

When you've got a firm offer, think about the future, not just the present. Will you, for example, be promoted for doing a good job, or will you have to compete with others? Know what success on the job means and where it can lead before you accept. Keep in mind that being hired in some circumstances is no guarantee of permanence.

When the negotiations are resolved, get the terms in writing if you can. If your employer does not provide this, write a letter to him or her summarizing your understanding of the terms and benefits. This will help protect you if for some reason the agreement made when you were hired isn't kept.

If you aren't offered the job, see if you can find out why—ideally from the person who interviewed you or who ultimately made the hiring decision. Some constructive criticism could prove very useful as you continue your job search.

OVERWHELMED? HERE'S YOUR BASIC HOMEWORK

Does this all seem daunting? It needn't be. Your job search will no doubt go very smoothly if you've taken the time to do the following basic homework before you start pounding the pavement.

Knowing Your Skills. Make an inventory of the skills you have to offer simply by listing for yourself (1) skills you've had a long time and feel confident about, (2) skills you've recently acquired, (3) skills you most enjoy using (some of 1 plus 2), and (4) skills you want to develop so that you can perform better in your current or next position.

Knowing Where You Want to Work. Decide where you want to work (with a public agency, a consulting firm, an advocacy group, and so on). List job types or tasks you would like to undertake (even if you're not sure you're totally ready for them yet).

Knowing How Your Skills and the Job Match Up. Finally, consider how you will answer basic questions about your experience, education, values, life goals, and skills when you are selected for an interview. Be prepared to answer the most basic
questions of all (which may be asked directly or hidden in other
questions): "What can you do for us?" and "Why should I hire
you?" To answer these, you will need to know something about
yourself and about the agency or firm interviewing you. Find out
about your prospective employer before the interview. Be prepared with your own questions to ask during the interview. And
think about how to orient your answers to the employer's needs
while also cogently and persuasively describing and selling your
skills and other attributes. Do not assume your resume will do
this job for you. All it does is get you into the interview.

The two most basic questions that will be on the job inter-viewer's mind are "What can you do for us?" and "Why should I hire you?"

4

What to Expect
From Your Job

Now that you've finally got that job, you will start learning what it really is. This chapter will give you some clues on what to expect. Here is the first clue: While you may have completed your formal education, you will probably find that a new form of education—involving politics, strategic planning, human behavior, and interpersonal relations—is just beginning.

UPON ARRIVING AT YOUR NEW JOB

Upon arriving at your new job, you should do the following:

- Confirm your salary, benefit plans, conditions of employment, rules about hours to be worked, and other such fundamentals. (If you think that at about age 25 it is absurdly premature to be thinking about such matters as retirement benefits, you have not been awake and become aware of what's going on in this society. Ask anyone age 35 or over.)

- Secure a copy of your organization's mission statement or legislative mandate to find out what it is supposed to be doing and its *raison d'être*.

- Ask for an overall orientation about the organization, but never assume you will be told everything all at once. Be continuously inquisitive. Read and become familiar with all recent reports (of major consequence), plans, programs, relevant ordinances, organization charts, work programs, annual reports, budgets, samples of published work, and so on. Become familiar with what is being done and for whom, what priorities prevail, who is in charge, and where the power lies within the agency or firm and within the community for which you work. By all means be guided by the section in Chapter 5 of this book entitled "Who Is The Client?"

- Talk to and quiz fellow workers about the workings and quirks of the organization, its employees and bosses, and its clients. (The answers will emerge slowly over time.)

- Find out about the different agencies or firms with which your organization interacts, and why.

- Go to a board or commission meeting and observe how your client, your boss, and the decision-makers behave, and what they are doing. There is much to learn by doing so, and some of what you learn will be essential at one point or another in your tenure or career.

- Subscribe to and read the local newspaper(s) or other relevant publications, including those that may report ill on your organization.

- Hang out in the local coffee shop from time to time, and chat with and listen to the local characters and the real people.

YOUR WORKPLACE: INSIDERS AND OUTSIDERS

Your workplace is not just the desk where you sit every day. You will be part of a larger organization, a group of people that may operate like a winning team or a dysfunctional family, or both, depending on the day, the circumstances, and the personalities involved. These people—your group of insiders—will be the ones who promote, evaluate, direct, work with, befriend, and gossip about you. Depending on the size and type of organization you work for, insiders might include:

- A principal, CEO, director, or department head,

- His or her administrators,

- Your immediate supervisor,

- Your co-workers, and

- Support staff (clerical, purchasing, office management, etc.).

You and your insider group might deal with, serve, or contend with any number of outsiders. Depending on where you work, they might include any of the following:

- People from other departments within your organization,

- Elected officials,

- Citizen boards and commissions,

- People representing other public or private organizations (government agencies, consulting firms, etc.),

- Private or nonprofit special interest groups and their representatives, and

- The general public.

As a rule of thumb, it's best to consider everyone on this list important in some way. Obviously, you will want to impress a director or department head, or your immediate supervisor. But the director's assistant may have more clout than your immediate supervisor in assessing whether you are fitting into the organization adequately. And he or she may be getting much of his or her information about you from clerical people you've treated well (or badly). Similarly, you never know when someone who is an outsider might have the ear of someone in your insider group.

Perhaps the following advice will help you pass through the probationary fire among all these strangers you will be working with.

The Planner as Nuisance

Within an organization, the planner, although not necessarily alone, may be well-equipped to hold decision-makers' feet to the fire, or to remind others to adhere honestly to existing policies and regulations, or to think new thoughts and do things in new ways. Often others will consider such behavior bothersome, but someone has to be the office nuisance.

TIPS FOR DEALING WITH INSIDERS

Support Staff

Don't underestimate the value of support staff. These people can be great allies, and provide you with important insights and information. They might also have the power to undermine your efforts if they take a dislike to you. Treat them with understanding and respect.

Find out who gives the support staff their work assignments, and work with the system that prevails. Sometimes (especially in a large organization) that system will be cumbersome and inefficient, but the time for reform will come later, when you are fully accepted or want to issue a parting statement when you leave for greener pastures.

You may encounter an overworked office manager who will purchase office supplies only after receiving a direct order from the director (only on Tuesdays). Or a word processing supervisor who will take work assignments only after being instructed by the director, who, being new to the job, usually waffles about deadlines, changing them frequently without telling the word processing supervisor.

Situations like these are quite common and often lead to conflict with the support people who take orders from one group but also work for another. Be sympathetic to their plight. Don't assume that your work is as important to them as it is to you. If you have to work through a supervisor to get the work assignment placed, then go through channels. Don't ever short-cut lines of authority with the support staff by just dumping an assignment on them and telling them you need it back this afternoon.

Do your part to develop working relationships with support staff that are based on mutual respect. For example:

- Always write out what you want done, rather than assuming the support person should know this or should come to you for direction. Is the report a draft or a final version? How many copies? When does it need to go out? Who gets the original copies? And so on. If there's a rush, be sure it's a real one, get the material to the support staff as soon as you can, be aware of their work schedules and conflicting deadlines, and be sure they understand the need for the rush.

- If a more formal approach is necessary, make your agreement on how and when by writing a memo on what you agreed to do. Ask to be notified immediately if something comes up to change this "contract." Better yet, keep an eye on the progress others are making. Don't be caught by surprise.

- When you are familiar with why the system was established the way it is, you might start tactfully working to improve it. For example, the word processing supervisor may insist that no one talk directly to his or her staff, for fear that "too much talk" will keep the staff from meeting deadlines. If this supervisor can learn to see the report production work as part of a critical path, however, he or she might realize that it is logical to schedule conferences between the report writer and the person who is responsible for report production. These conferences could take the form of checkpoints on the schedule. Once the supervisor realizes that contact between the writer and the production people is going to be structured and work-related, he or she might agree to modify the top-down direction of the arrows and permit some lateral contact.

A Planner's Best Friends

There are usually one or two people in any office on whom the very conduct of your working life may depend. These people may include office managers, secretaries, word processing people or data entry clerks, administrative assistants, the money people, or the graphics specialists. They will not have planning educations or the skills you possess, but they are the glue that holds a department or agency together. They hold and exercise a kind of power that you need to get accustomed to for your own well-being. They regard themselves as essential to the smooth working of the office—and rightfully so. At times they are rushed, under stress, and fragile. They may require occasional expressions of gratitude. You must court their favor, so that when you really need them in order to get your project completed properly and on time they will be there for you—and because it is the right thing to do.

Other Co-Workers

People on the same "level" as you at work can be your natural allies—you often share common education, duties, and perspectives on your organization. They might also be your closest competitors. A friendly-but-businesslike approach is best, at least until you get a better sense of individual personalities.

One of the hardest things for many people to learn after they leave school is how to be a team player with co-workers. To do this, it's important to recognize that any group charged with a task to perform together has an internal agenda to cover first: the group process, or how to create and maintain a group that functions productively. This means first considering what each of you can do to help others feel valued and genuinely enthusiastic about achieving your common goals. It also means recognizing what each person's contribution can be, and identifying ways to remove any obstacles to each person's performance so that the group accomplishes its goals as efficiently as possible.

Work teams or task forces of co-workers are often leaderless. While opinion is divided on whether it's really necessary to select a leader, group members will often assign themselves individual roles. Here are some examples:

Task Roles:

1. Initiating (tasks, goals, ideas, etc).

2. Information- or opinion-seeking.

3. Clarifying (clearing confusions, giving examples, etc).

4. Playing the "devil's advocate" (exercising caution, testing ideas for strength in face of expected opposition).

5. Consensus-testing (checking for agreement).

6. Summarizing (pulling ideas together, identifying who agreed to do what, and by when).

Group Maintenance Roles:

1. Harmonizing (reducing tension, getting people to explore differences).

2. Encouraging (giving positive strokes).

3. Expressing group feelings (sensing moods and relationships within the group).

4. Setting standards (expressing standards for the group to keep).

5. Compromising (suggesting means to resolve polarized positions on issues).

6. Gatekeeping (keeping everyone involved; usually the chairperson's role).

Negative Roles (which the group must police):

1. Distracting (hair-splitting, anecdote-spinning, and so on).

2. Topic-jumping (not staying on the subject).

3. Playing the cynic ("What can we do?" "It's no use trying, we'll only get overruled . . ." and so on).

4. Continuous talking (carrying on a monologue).

5. Withdrawing.

6. Constant, irrelevant horsing around (often masks contempt for the group task, or some other dysfunction).

7. Playing manipulative games (using others for self-interest, one-upmanship).

Note: If these problems persist, consider talking with the troublemakers (and/or their supervisor) privately. Your office may also want to bring in group counselors to conduct team-building exercises.

No one plays all of these roles, nor does anyone usually play the same role all the time. Paying attention to which ones you—and your co-workers—typically play can help you do your job better and further the group's goals.

You may encounter behavior among co-workers that does not seem productive. Examples:

"Us Against Them." Sometimes a group becomes so cohesive that its members hesitate to speak critically; instead, they smooth over debate, avoid responsibility, and rationalize their (often forced) consensus as being "morally right." This leads to an "us against them" attitude toward others not in the group.

"Empire Building." Many organizations contain people who have carved out their own little empires and will not cooperate on anything that threatens their status quo, whether it's changing "the way things have always been done," or taking on new work. Sometimes the best you can do is to work around these people— and try not to start behaving this way yourself.

Your Immediate Supervisor

It is vital to stay on the right side of your immediate supervisor, who will conduct the most critical evaluations of your perform- ance. This person may be sizing you up based on a wide range of criteria (see "Department Administrators" below). Doing good work is necessary; however, most people are discharged because of undesirable behavior or character traits rather than a lack of skills. And while government agencies cannot fire with the ease of private sector or nonprofit organizations, they do practice sub- tle forms of "dehiring" (transfers-that-equal-banishment, lack of promotion, etc.) with people who have these deficiencies.

Your supervisor is a human being, some- one with his or her own tendencies and quirks.

There is no way to assure that you will register positively with a boss without "kissing up" to him or her. Perhaps the best advice is first to recognize that your supervisor is a human being— someone with his or her own tendencies and quirks, who is nei- ther all bad nor all good, and who may have his or her own boss to contend with, maybe even unhappily at times. Part of your job is to make this person look good. To do this, you will want to learn how your boss operates, and how you can fit into that sys- tem most usefully. You may find that the system your boss uses is not the one you would design, or the one that makes best use of your skills. Again, try to adapt until you are respected enough to make (helpful) suggestions. Your boss will most likely value your independent thinking on all matters—even when you dis- agree—provided that you present your ideas constructively.

No boss will be able to read your mind—or vice versa. It always pays to review with your supervisor what his or her expectations are of you for each work assignment. You will also be responsi- ble for speaking up when you are "getting into trouble," whether that's becoming mired in a research problem, doing work that is beyond your expertise, becoming so overloaded that you are in danger of missing deadlines, or confronting a difficult situation with others outside your agency or department.

The Principal, CEO, Director, or Department Head

If the ultimate boss (principal of the firm, CEO, director, department head, city manager) is not your immediate supervisor as well, he or she will probably be more remote. In very large organizations, you may see this person only on such ceremonial occasions as staff meetings, budget sessions, presentations at public meetings, or office parties.

Meetings where the No. 1 is present can be anxiety-ridden for novices. You might find yourself backed into a tight corner when you are asked a question or when you meet unexpected opposition to something you said. In these situations, you have essentially two choices: (a) Admit you don't know something, and offer to get the information after the meeting; or (b) try to come up with some sort of response, and correct yourself after the meeting if necessary. (Your supervisor should not let you get into this kind of fix, and should come to your rescue if necessary.)

Difficult as it can be, you will need to remember "your place." Despite the rhetoric, most work places are not egalitarian democracies. Points to keep in mind for getting along with directors and department heads are:

- Managers give opinions, other workers (you) give information and sometimes advice, and the director makes the decision.

- It's best not to speak at group meetings with the chief unless you have something to say. Don't use the director's time unless it's absolutely necessary.

- If you want the director to set your project in motion, get the background work done and have it ready for his or her okay or signature in the form of a finished product (letter, resolution, agenda, etc.).

- It's best not to bypass your immediate supervisor in any dealings with the director (whether it's taking directions or providing information) unless you are told it's okay to do so.

Department Administrators

Larger organizations, especially governmental ones, may also have department administrators who are charged with keeping the agency machinery working. These people are responsible for evaluating your performance and for making salary and promotion recommendations to the director or department head. Administrators usually need to get answers to the following questions to evaluate you as a new or probationary employee:

1. *Volume of acceptable work completed.* Do you consistently accomplish a day's work for a day's pay?

2. *Meeting deadlines.* Do you make an honest attempt to meet deadlines and give advance notice when you can't?

3. *Job skill level.* Do you consistently demonstrate the skills needed to carry out your job? Is your work accurate and complete, or does it have to be redone?

4. *Oral and written expression.* Do you have the ability to communicate effectively with fellow workers and others, both one-on-one and in meetings?

5. *Attendance and reliability in work hours.* Are you getting famous for long lunches, overly lengthy field trips, late arrivals, mental health days, or missed meetings and appointments?

6. *Taking direction.* Are you enthusiastic, or at least agreeable, about the work assigned to you, or do you constantly whine and bicker about job assignments? Do you ask relevant questions, or do you accept faulty instructions passively without a full understanding of what you're supposed to do?

7. *Planning and organization.* Do you plan and organize the steps on an assigned job to achieve the required results on time? Or do you attack the work thoughtlessly, or with such blind enthusiasm that mistakes occur and deadlines are missed?

8. *Getting along with others.* Do you look for ways to bring out the best in your co-workers? Or are you a disruptive influence? Do you lower the morale of your co-workers by constant griping? Do you bother them with your personal problems, and so on?

9. *Meeting and handling outsiders.* Does your contact with people from outside the organization (through personal or telephone conversations, written correspondence, day-to-day public appearances, meetings) promote a good image of the agency you represent?

10. *Performance in new situations.* Do you accept change willingly or slow it down by resistance or lack of flexibility?

11. ***Performance under stress.*** Can you work effectively in situations where pace, pressure, and tempo are demanding? Can you respond productively in an emergency?

12. ***Going beyond the call of duty.*** Do you suggest new ideas that might help the organization? Are you on the lookout for useful information, contacts, and so on?

13. ***Overall attitude.*** Do you work with other people in a positive, constructive way? Do you smile? Do you look after your appearance and dress appropriately? (This is a reminder that everything counts.)

Administrators may get answers to these questions through their own observations, by interviewing people in contact with you, and by keeping track of complaints, foul-ups, and so on. If your organization does not have a departmental administrator, responsibility for this type of review will usually fall to your immediate supervisor. Keeping these factors in mind can help you meet your employer's expectations.

TIPS FOR DEALING WITH OUTSIDERS

People from outside of your organization will judge you on how well you present yourself—and how well (or badly) you represent your agency or organization. The best way to present yourself will differ according to whom you work for, and which type of group you are addressing. Here are some general observations.

People from Other Departments or Agencies

If you work for a large organization, you may occasionally seek the cooperation of a decision-maker or staff person in another department within the organization, or staff in an agency at another level of government. Regardless of where you work, you will probably at some point need something from an outside agency. Perhaps your department or group needs matching services for a federal grant, or a review of an environmental impact report by a certain date. Perhaps you are contracting with a consulting firm for a special study. Or perhaps you work for a consulting firm or a nonprofit, and need information from a government agency or

When you need something from an outside agency, you will be conducting diplomatic negotiations with a sovereign entity.

from another consultant. Or perhaps your agency is developing a new program that requires a joint effort among two or more agencies and their professional and administrative staff representatives.

In any of these instances, you are conducting diplomatic negotiations with a sovereign entity. As in any negotiation, you will want to have a firm grasp of what your organization needs from this outside entity, and when. You will also need to know what is important to that entity, what their standard operating procedure is, and how they are likely to view you.

If you are making a request, you may want to have a good argument for why they would benefit from cooperating, and how much authority goes with any responsibility (does their name appear in the report, will they be quoted, and so on). Remember, some personality types in some situations thrive on holding their information close to their chests, not wanting to share or needing to maintain their power at the expense of being cooperative or gracious. In large venues this can be commonplace.

"Tact is ...a kind of mindreading."
—Sarah Orne Jewett (1849-1909), American writer

Provided there are no real or perceived conflicts of interest, it can be useful to cultivate a friend in an outside entity that you deal with regularly, someone you can contact on an informal basis. This person can keep track of information sources, help you set up meetings, feed you inside intelligence, and so on. It's also good to try to have an ample supply of "carrots and sticks." Think about what you can offer this outside agency in return, and how you can prod them when necessary.

Consultants

Consultant relations is a specialized area of knowledge. Whether you are hiring a consulting firm or working for one yourself, you will learn how to function in this arena through experience and by watching your more seasoned co-workers. You might also consult books and other references that specifically address this subject. Generally, if you hire a consulting firm, that firm is there to help you; conversely, if you work for a consulting firm, your job is to make your clients happy. The intent is to create a mutually beneficial relationship.

The interests of the consultant and the client do occasionally clash, however. A consultant might balk at taking on the work you need done for the price you can afford to pay; or your client might put pressure on you to make a report recommendation that you do not believe is appropriate. Under these circumstances, learning the art of negotiation—and knowing your limits—becomes all-important. Many of the suggestions for interagency relations offered above also apply to transactions involving consultants.

Individual Citizens and Citizens Groups

Private citizens and citizens groups may not fully understand who you are and what you do. They may be suspicious of you, particularly if you work for a government agency, a consulting firm, or a real estate developer—or if you appear young and "wet behind the ears." The most important things to remember in dealing with these people are to listen attentively, to express ideas as clearly and forthrightly as possible, and to avoid being defensive or argumentative.

Citizen groups may include general or neighborhood interest groups, citizens' advisory committees, and homeowners' associations. Most of the time, your dealings with these groups will be in the form of meetings held to present information and elicit feedback. Since the main purpose of these meetings is communication, they should be open and reasonably well structured so that everyone present will be able to speak without hindrance and feel comfortable doing so. (For more on this matter, see Chapter 8, Essential Political Skills.)

Your role at these meetings will vary according to whether you're a government employee, a private-sector developer or consultant, or a nonprofit representative. As a general rule, whoever is in charge of the meeting should announce what the meeting is for, give the ground rules for public participation, and explain who you are and what you've got to accomplish. If you're only there for fact-finding, exploration, or to listen, this should be pointed out, so that you won't get the pressure or venom that the group has been saving for the politicians or other easy targets.

Regardless of your role, be careful and ready to back up everything you say. "Winging it" is generally not advised. You are acting as a diplomatic emissary of your organization. If you goof in some way, people at the top will hear about it directly, and retribution will magnify as it filters down to you. Therefore, it's important for you to do thorough homework on what your specific mission is, whether that's to communicate information or agency policy, get responses to options, priorities, objectives, or whatev-

Being diplomatic means never having to say you're sorry.

er. Have some idea of what your supervisor would consider to be the preferred results of a successful meeting. Being diplomatic means never having to say you're sorry.

If you are a local government planner working with a citizens advisory committee, you may serve as temporary staff to this group, often in liaison with a consultant or people from another agency. Your responsibilities may include preparing findings and recommendations in the form of a report. Careful listening, facilitating clear opinions, and getting things down in language designed to capture the feeling of what was said are among the important skills needed. Other necessary skills include genuinely involving citizens in the creative work of policy- and plan-making—not as passive participants but as thinkers and workers. To do this well is an art, and your abilities will improve with practice.

Special Interest Organizations

Such groups as chambers of commerce, unions, nonprofit environmental groups, and associations of farmers or builders are essentially protective organizations for the benefit of their members. Thus, they take stands on whether or not a proposal is good or bad from their particular perspective. These may be rigid, ideological positions—but with some flexibility built in. For example, the construction unions may be on strike against the builders, but the unions may still offer to support a big development project at public hearings because the project will provide more construction jobs.

Often there is an anti-special-interest group involved in the same issue, so someone looking for middle ground can be caught in the crossfire. For example, nonprofit organizations that advocate affordable housing and jobs might be pitted against environmental groups that want to slow down growth and keep many developable areas open. Often these groups have their own staff and fact-finding capabilities (and you could be a member of their staff one day). You can be sure they possess well-honed political skills.

Again, your dealings with special interest groups will vary according to whom you work for. You may be employed by one of these groups yourself, or you may come into contact with them as a representative of government, a consulting firm, or a real estate developer. Regardless of which side you are on, make sure that any work you present is accurate, to avoid being challenged and embarrassed by someone else's conflicting data. It's also good to remember that special interest groups often believe they are on a mission, and generally do not see their positions as being open for debate. Therefore, unless you yourself work for the group (and perhaps even if you do), you should avoid being drawn into ideological battles that are unlikely to change anyone's mind. Try to focus the discussion on the problem at hand and possible solutions. It's the job of others to sort out and deal with the ideological differences and issues of community values.

Appointed Boards and Commissions

Most boards and commissions are made up of laypeople, and are charged with making recommendations to an elected body. In the nonprofit world, boards of directors make decisions on behalf of the nonprofit organization they oversee.

Many board and commission members may be surprisingly (to you) ill-equipped to handle their jobs due to lack of training, orientation, and experience. It's important to keep this in mind in your dealings with them. Remember that they are volunteering their time. Be informative but respectful (not condescending), and do not ridicule or overcompensate for such shortcomings. Also, remember that their roles are advisory, and rarely are they charged with making final and binding decisions. At times they will be overridden by elected officials, which tends to make them cranky.

In particular, if you are a staff person to such a body, it's important not to become their guru. Keeping these lay members in a dependency state may boost your ego, but it's bad for the public interest (or, in the case of a nonprofit, the organization's interest) because you are not supposed to do their job for them. What they bring to the decision- and policy-making process is their sense of values. They can evaluate, for example, whether a proposal will benefit all the citizens of the community. Your judgment should not be substituted for theirs at this level. As with the citizens advisory committee, your staff role is to facilitate their making reasoned, fact-based recommendations. You should act as educator, data gatherer, issue interpreter, plus sounding board for the technical feasibility of their ideas. And, do not be surprised if you discover that there are political goings-on in such groups, which are often basic training grounds for entering elected politics at a later date.

Elected Officials

Because elected officials usually have only a very limited time to spend on many of the things that come before them, they often have only a hazy grasp of the details. Therefore, they will use their heads for what they know best—assessing the political pros and cons of the issue—and may tend to hold the rational, objective recommendations of technical people at arm's length. Meetings are formal, structured, and legalistic. Political advisors or aides work under great handicaps. Agendas are usually overfull, meetings and hearings inevitably run later than scheduled, and more people want to speak than time allows. So while you may have rehearsed a brilliant 20-minute presentation with maps, charts, tables, and written reports, you may find that you will have to get the message across in the three minutes before bids for a park concession are opened. (It's natural to think that what you've labored on for months is the most important matter on the agenda; elected officials may not agree, however, particularly if it's a "bad news" item that's likely to cause more political grief than joy.)

This means that, regardless of whom you represent, you will want to be prepared with a scaled-back version of your presentation to an elected body; that way you won't stumble and fumble if asked to edit your remarks down to a summary on a moment's notice. You may also want to avoid going in with only one option, especially on a controversial matter. Even if you are the staff to this elected group, keep in mind that politicians often use staff people's recommendations as foils in structuring more politically appealing compromises. You will want to avoid being caught in the middle, and coming off looking unreasonable, pompous, or rigid, while the politicians appear humane and diplomatic. If you keep your options at the ready, you won't be frozen out of compromise decisions. It's important to remember that your first-choice approach may not be the only one, and others may want to work on the solution, too.

It doesn't hurt to keep in mind that on some occasions elected officials will display hostility toward or fear of you, or will cower when forced to face an angry crowd of citizens. Their behavior under such stressful circumstances cannot be predicted, and may not be pretty. You'd best be ready to accept even bizarre behaviors and to adapt to the situation as it unfolds if this sort of thing happens on your watch or in your presence.

EXPECT THE UNEXPECTED

Inevitably, things happen on the job that are not predictable and may alter what at the outset seemed to be a stable, exciting, and organized venue for the initiation of your professional career. Among the possibilities are:

- The boss retires, is fired or is promoted upward;

- The boss's boss withdraws funds and your job is reduced or eliminated;

- The politics change due to an election, and planning goals or priorities are modified or replaced by new ones;

- There's a departmental reorganization and the chain of command changes; or

- A co-worker gets sick, quits, or is transferred, and you have to do his or her work as well as your own.

While these things may not be predictable, they need not come as a total surprise. Keeping your "ear to the ground" and following the guidelines for workplace relations offered in this chapter may help you anticipate and prepare for these upheavals.

"We trained hard—but every time we were beginning to form up in teams, we would be reorganized. I was to learn later in life that we tend to meet any new situation by reorganizing—and a wonderful method it can be for creating the illusion of progress while producing inefficiency and demoralization."
—Petronius (d. A.D. 66)

5

For Whom Are You Working?

A s you begin your new job, you will be focused on the work at hand, and probably will be very grateful for a job at all after a lengthy search, especially if the fit seems just right for you. And yet you may not know much about the fundamental characteristics of workplaces and about the people with whom you will be working. The first four chapters of this book attempted to give you some basic background information and some clues about what to expect from your first professional or pre-professional job.

Before setting forth more explicit guidelines on developing your career (Part II), it is worth pausing to consider three areas of overriding concern to anyone embarking on a professional life within the planning milieu: understanding the organizational culture of which you are a part, sharpening your perceptions of who you really will be working for (i.e., who the "client" is), and recognizing ethical issues that may arise as you pursue your life's work.

THE AGENCY OR COMPANY CULTURE

T he day your new job begins, you become a member of an organization that has its own unique culture. No two organizations are alike, and the traditional organization chart tells you virtually nothing about how the organization works, how well or badly its members function together, or whether the organization is productive and a joyful place to spend 35 or more hours in each week, not to mention additional hours attending evening meetings. Because work in any organization should be engaging and satisfying, it is in everyone's interest to understand the organization's culture and to learn how to deal with it and, if necessary, improve it.[1]

"Culture" is what people do together; it is the sum of the agency's or firm's ideas, interests, values, and attitudes. It consists of the members' backgrounds, traditions, myths, fears, biases, ideologies, aspirations, skills, and expectations. Your organization's culture reflects how people working there feel about doing their jobs. The health of an organization's culture can tell you a lot about how well the organization functions. And, how well it functions can tell you a lot about its culture, whether the odds of succeeding in its mission are excellent or dismal, and whether you will be content and highly motivated—or miserable.

When you are on the job awhile, take a look at the culture in which you find yourself. First, assume that the organization's culture is an intricate pattern of how people do things. Observe who is rewarded and who is penalized—or ignored. If the organization is divided into sections or departments, how does each view the other and behave as a result?

The group culture will be transmitted through dress, style, language (what is said and what is not—and how), jokes, gossip, who has and who exercises power and influence and how they do it. Remember that all (or almost all) of these people are fundamentally the same as you—no worse and no better. They are merely acting according to the culture of the organization and according to the situation in which they find themselves.

Bosses inevitably have the most influence over an organization's culture. If your boss behaves with intelligence and in caring ways, so will others. If he or she behaves aggressively or with indifference, or perhaps passively and without energy and passion, so will others. If the boss wants people to cooperate and to be productive, he or she must be cooperative and productive. Bosses set the stage. Good bosses (and even bad ones) are worth observing and learning from, especially since sooner of later you are likely to become a boss within your own work culture.

The early stages of your career are the points in time to set some standards, based in part on understanding how organizations function. These standards can govern your own role in and influence over creating the right environment in which to function professionally and with satisfaction.

While much significance is placed on productivity in private companies, no public agency can be doing its job well without a similar focus. Successful companies have high productivity, safety, employee satisfaction, and resilience. So, too, should all public enterprises.

If an organization's culture is the intricate pattern of how people do things individually and together, and for the common good, or in pursuit of the organization's mission, then it is also true that for some organizations, and especially for some public agencies, the culture may not be as mature (i.e., open-minded, diverse, directed, humane) as one might wish.[2] There are likely to be obstacles to overcome and challenges to face. These include but are not limited to the following:

"Creative minds have always been known to survive any kind of bad training." —Anna Freud (1895-1982), Austrian psychoanalyst

- There is often a big gap between what you think ought to be done and what you will be allowed to do. Maybe you can do something about this, maybe not.

- There are often real lapses in competence within the workplace, and very often these are at the management level. The larger the agency, the more likely this will be so.

- You will have these stunning awakenings from time to time: that the organization's modus operandi really consists of muddling through; that it is a wonder that anything gets done; that you can easily become part of the problem; and that all agencies are dysfunctional in one way or another at one time or another, at least in part even if not entirely—notwithstanding that there are well-recognized ways to correct most situations leading to dysfunction if only someone on high would initiate them.

- There are difficult people in this world, and they may end up at the desk next to yours or as your boss. You may be managed by or be obliged to work with fellow professionals or decision-makers who don't know what they are doing, or lack qualities and skills that are obviously needed for the role they have been asked to play.

Notwithstanding these apparent negative traits of immature work cultures, there are ways to make your mark in any setting. There are always jobs to be done, progress to be made, clients to be satisfied, and opportunities for those who are looking for them. The possibilities worth being aware of include:

- Organizations of all kinds do respect and appreciate initiative and new ideas. It may take some time to figure out who elects to listen to you, and much skill may be required to communicate your ideas without threatening others. Knowing how to communicate well and effectively is equivalent to being a great surgeon—knowing what you want to do and then knowing how to do it.

- Finding kindred souls within your agency and/or in another agency with whom you can work cooperatively is essential in order to nurture respect, test ideas, and plot strategies—and it works.

- Invariably, and especially when you are the sole planner in an office or on a multi-disciplinary team, your ability to think conceptually and to formulate policies, implementation measures, and actions will distinguish you from others and may make you highly regarded and marketable. You will probably develop a reputation for being able to put diverse pieces of a puzzle together, synthesize and assemble a lot of data, findings, and recommendations, write policy and planning proposals that are accompanied by action plans, and put all of this into one package. And those skills, which you will very likely find out are quite rare, may turn out to be your trump card, the thing no one else can do and the mark of your career.

- Learning and practicing consensus-building, working out compromises, and brokering deals, whether in your office, in an interagency setting, or in a politicized setting, are paths to becoming effective in the workplace and a successful practitioner. Few people do this well.

- If you can write well, design or illustrate well, or manage a group or public meeting well, or you move into a supervisory or management position and perform well there, you can be assured that you will mark your place in the scheme of things and bring credit to your employer.

- Another way you can establish your reputation is by knowing how to work effectively with your client so that he or she gets the best out of you and you get the best out of your client in terms of direction and support.

WHO IS THE CLIENT?

One of the stickier puzzles for the newly appointed at any level of seniority is figuring out who the client is. First, you may justifiably be wondering what is meant by "client"; the definition of the term can vary according to whether you work for a public agency (where it may not be obvious), a nonprofit, or a private firm doing work for a public agency. In this section we will try to unravel the puzzle and give you some insights and guidelines about the concept of the "client" and what it can mean to you in the practice of planning.

You may think the client is your immediate supervisor, the person who directs you and holds some power over you and your future. He or she is the person to whom you report, and who tells you what to do, judges your work, and has a big say in your prospects for promotion. And so on up the line. In an agency with an obvious chain of command, your immediate supervisor may in fact be your client—although we are about to show you that even this may not be entirely the case.

The client dilemma is typically most puzzling if you work for a public agency, or in any situation where you are employed directly or indirectly by a firm on contract to a public agency. In these cases, the reality that there is more than one client makes the job tougher, the demands on you greater, and the need for education (generalist skills), a general understanding about how our culture works, and some considerable amount of perspective, essential. You will need to think carefully to identify the client or clients, and then figure out how to work with and satisfy them.

To understand one's responsibility to the client or clients, and the challenges involved, consider the situation of a private-sector consultant hired by a local government. While it is quite clear to the city manager or planning director who the immediate client of the just-hired consultant is—it is one of them or both—their own client is the elected city council to whom they report and at whose sufferance they serve. They are not about to have the hired consultant misunderstand who is in charge, and yet it is often the case that the consultant perceives the true client to be the elected officials or, rightfully so, perhaps those who "hire" the elected officials: the citizenry. If this is the case, life gets complicated for all concerned.

A planning consultant is often hired to give an independent opinion or recommendation unfettered by the issues of employment security that come with being a city manager or planning director. Consultants try to weigh not only what the city manager, planning director, and hiring legislative body say they want done, but also other considerations such as unintended consequences and impacts, the needs and wants of the general public, the expectations of the business community, the long-term general welfare, perhaps even mandates from the courts. And they try to do so objectively and free of spontaneous or gratuitous directions from and interference by the legislators.

In asserting this kind of independence, consultants run up against a dilemma: For whose benefit am I crafting policy recommendations and plans, and by whom and by whose preferences, values, and ideas am I most guided? Is it the planning director's, the city manager's—who are charged with overseeing my work? Is it their boss the legislative body, or maybe just a majority of three out of five? Or, is it the 21-member citizens advisory committee with whom I have been working for the past year? If the latter, do they really represent the citizenry or merely the most elite, the most active, the most verbal, and the most politically savvy and insistent? And do any of the above speak for the kids or the as-yet-unborn kids of the kids? Or the endangered species? Or the mandates of the state legislature or the courts?

Figuring all this out and plotting a correct path is a challenge that can only be learned on the job. The rules and realities of the game will change with each venue, context, or project in which you find yourself.

Perhaps a true story can best illustrate the points set forth above. The names of the actors have been changed to protect the guilty and the innocent alike. The venue is a suburban city in the middle of the incipient environmental movement of the 1970s when old-time politicians were being replaced with a wave of environmentalists and government reformers.

A True Story

After a competitive selection process, consultant Ace Goodman executed a contract with the City of Sutter Point (population 75,000) to undertake, manage, and complete a comprehensive land-use plan. The contract was between the Sutter Point city council and Goodman and included requirements that (1) Goodman help organize a citizens advisory committee chosen by the city council, and (2) he report to and directly work with the city planning director, who was also directed to facilitate data collection, map preparation, meetings with various city staff, and meetings with a citizens advisory committee.

All went well for a few months, but then difficulties arose. Ace and the city planning director experienced a tense working relationship. Although this was manageable, Ace determined that the director had limited credibility in city hall and especially with the city council, and not much among the public. As one must in the role of consultant, Ace Goodman had to decide whether the druthers of the director, the putative client, were to be taken seriously.

Ace judged that he needed to identify an alternative client. Among the obvious candidates was the city planning commission, a group of appointed citizens whose adoption of policies and plans at some later date was mandated by law. There were problems here, too, because the chairman of the planning commission was hostile to the very idea of the city engaging in any sort of intervention in the real estate market place. It followed that he was hostile to the consultant's role. This growing tension set up a battle, played out in public, between the newly elected "environmentalist" city council majority and the majority on the planning commission over what ideas would govern the plan-making being attempted by the consultant.

Goodman was placed at a great disadvantage in not knowing who was in charge, how the battle was going to play out, and whose ideas to subscribe to and reflect in the plan-making activity. Thus, how to settle on who the client was or might turn out to be became the central issue.

Concurrently, the citizens advisory committee (CAC) was getting organized, feeling its oats, and asserting itself as an actor among the others. Another dynamic was that several members of the CAC were more articulate and smarter than almost anyone on the city planning commission, tended to be allies of the new majority on the city council, and were excited by the prospect of wresting control out of the hands of the planning commission and making the upcoming plan "their" plan. Some were also interested in the idea of running for and gaining seats on the planning commission and then, one day, on the city council.

At this juncture, Ace Goodman had to weigh whether it was best to please and be directed by the planning commission, the city council, or the CAC. That is, who was the true client—not in terms of who paid the bill, but whose ideas and preferences were to be reflected in the plan. It was more than evident that plan-making was becoming political and that each group held distinctly different views about what was preferred policy for future growth and development within the planning area.

The choice for Goodman was to perceive the CAC as the new and true client, on the assumption that this group outnumbered, out-thought, and outwitted the weakened members of the planning commission and the old-timers on the city council and were the new force in town or soon would be. He also thought the CAC best represented what the changing community wanted and was going to demand by ballot box sooner or later.

The upshot was that Ace had a client with whom he could work and had clear directions for crafting the plan. If Ace had adhered to established convention, he would have stuck with the planning director or the planning commission as client. In making the judgment he did, which was never articulated or even referred to in any public setting, he took the risk of alienating the planning director and the planning commission, which was, in fact, the outcome. But he counted his votes and when all was said and done, his choice of client was the correct one; the proposed plan, reflecting the goals and preferences of the CAC, sailed through to adoption and became the law of the land. In the process, the membership of the planning commission was altered to suit the new city council and the CAC.

There will be some who would argue that the role of the professional planner is to keep squeaky clean and well removed from these sorts of goings-on. After all, isn't planning supposed to be an objective, nonpolitical process? But the question arose about identifying the true client, and Ace Goodman had to find a way to adopt a stance, protect the plan-making process, proceed with the work under contract, and adapt to the political realities of the time and place. Ace was one of the actors in this drama, like it or not, and he could not remain strictly neutral and nonpolitical. All of this is part of the real world of planning and plan-making, and knowing your client is one of those skills worth learning.

ETHICAL ISSUES

The Definition of Ethics

The American Heritage Dictionary defines "ethics" as (1) the philosophy of morals, and (2) the rules or standards governing the conduct of the members of a profession.

As you no doubt realize by now, there is an inherent tension between the idealism of the planning profession and the pragmatism of politics. When planning and politics mix—and they do all the time, because political decisions are what make planning actually happen—questions of ethics and fairness often arise.

The subject of ethics is a tricky one. An action or decision that seems unfair, unreasonable, or unwise to you may not actually be unethical, at least as defined by the majority of your colleagues or by the community where you are working. That does not mean, though, that you must automatically ignore your feelings about the action or decision and move on. Often your own internal moral compass will be your best (and possibly only) guide to deciding what to do when you find yourself in a situation that offends your sense of ethical behavior.

You are not completely on your own, however. The American Institute of Certified Planners (AICP) maintains a Code of Ethics and Professional Conduct (see sidebar of excerpts). The code addresses the planner's responsibility to the public and the public interest, to clients and employers, to the profession and colleagues, and to himself or herself. AICP also issues advisory rulings on specific ethical questions and problems (such as sexual harassment, conflicts of interest, outside employment or moonlighting, and honesty in the use of information), and handles charges of alleged misconduct by AICP members. The code and its interpretation are subject to constant discussion and evolution. Contact the American Planning Association (APA) to find out the latest. You need not be an APA or AICP member to access this information on the APA web site (*www.planning.org*). Other associations, composed of people in allied professions with whom you work, also face ethical issues and maintain codes of ethics and professional conduct.

Excerpts from the AICP Code of Ethics

The Planner's Responsibility to the Public: A planner's primary obligation is to serve the public interest. While the definition of the public interest is formulated through continuous debate, a planner owes allegiance to a conscientiously attained concept of the public interest . . .

The Planner's Responsibility to Clients and Employers: A planner owes diligent, creative, independent and competent performance of work in pursuit of the client's or employer's interest. Such performance should be consistent with the planner's faithful service to the public interest.

The Planner's Responsibility to the Profession and to Colleagues: A planner should contribute to the development of the profession by improving knowledge and techniques, making work relevant to solutions of community problems, and increasing public understanding of planning activities. A planner should treat fairly the professional views of qualified colleagues and members of other professions.

The Planner's Self-Responsibility: A planner should strive for high standards of professional integrity, proficiency, and knowledge.

Source: American Institute of Certified Planners, AICP Code of Ethics and Professional Conduct, adopted October 1978, amended October 1991.

Some professional behavior is clearly unethical. Examples would include a planning director accepting cash from a real estate developer or a consultant in exchange for a political favor or a recommendation for project approval. Or that same planning director recommending approval of a development project in which he or she holds a financial interest. In these instances, the planning director is compromising his or her professional duties in favor of personal gain, not to mention risking going to jail. (And don't think these things don't happen.)

But what if the planning director occasionally—or even once—goes to lunch at the invitation of a real estate developer or a consultant who works in the community? These may be people with whom the planning director has worked in the past, regards well professionally, might even like personally, and in any case wants to stay on good terms with. What if the developer or consultant pays for lunch? Has the planning director accepted a "bribe"? What if a development project is proposed in the neighborhood where the planning director lives? The development might eventually affect property values in the neighborhood (or then again, it might not). Does that mean that the planning director has a conflict of interest if he or she makes a recommendation on the project? In these instances, the ethical line becomes much fuzzier. (Some jurisdictions require planning directors and other department heads to remove themselves from decisions involving their own neighborhoods.)

Or, to pose a situation that might arise for you in your first months or years on the job, what if your boss or client reverses a controversial recommendation in a report you have written? It may be that you got your facts wrong, in which case you are certainly not dealing with a question of ethics. Or, your boss or client may simply disagree with you, and believe that the decision-makers will, too. In this case, you are dealing with a difference in professional judgment, and possibly differences in values. These differences may cause you to feel that you, and the other people affected by the change in recommendation, are being treated unfairly and unreasonably, and you may question why you are working where you are. Even so, these may still be differences in basic attitudes and professional opinion that do not add up to a case of ethical misconduct.

On the other hand, you may suspect some kind of behind-the-scenes maneuvering, in which your boss or client is conspiring to withhold or alter important information—and in doing so is compromising some fundamental aspect of the "public interest," however that may be defined in this case. Here, you may be dealing with questions of ethics, although again the strength of your case depends not only on your own interpretation of the facts, but also the interpretations of your colleagues and the community where you are working. This is not an exact science.

Your best course of action is to talk about ethical questions with your colleagues—preferably before any dubious situations arise. Bring in a copy of the AICP Code of Ethics. (Again, you need not be an APA or AICP member to get this information from the APA web site (*www.planning.org*).) Find out if your organization has any adopted standards of its own (and if not, discuss whether they are needed). Pose questions about "what ifs." This is an area in which general pronouncements from on high are no substitute for case studies involving actual facts, interpretations from your colleagues, and an understanding of your geographic, organizational, or professional community.

"What is morality in any given time and place? It is what the majority then and there happen to like, and immorality is what they dislike."
—Alfred North Whitehead (1861-1947), English philosopher

If you are seriously considering blowing the whistle on perceived unethical behavior, make sure you fully understand the implications first. AICP or other professional organizations may be able to provide advice and guidance on what course you should take. It is wise to recognize that whistle-blowing can have long-term personal consequences; you could lose your job and find that you have a reputation as a troublemaker when you begin searching for a new one. In a truly egregious situation, taking this chance may appear to be the only conscientious choice. Just be sure you've done some thorough soul-searching before you act.

Notes

1. Credit for the basic ideas (about a company or agency culture) in this section go to Barry Phegan, whose seminal book, *Developing Your Company Culture, The Joy of Leadership—A Handbook For Leaders and Managers* (Context Press, 1994), is an eye-opener for anyone who is interested in figuring out how organizations work for better or for worse, and how to make them better. Although Phegan writes about corporate America, his lessons are relevant within public agency and nonprofit settings too.

2. Phegan argues that in mature organizations "employees at all levels experience trust and psychological safety. Rank, authority, and control issues do not dominate their landscapes. These companies (insert: agencies) see diversity of the work force as one reason for their success…Like a mature person (these companies) determine their own future and experience few limits…Success comes hand in hand with developing an engaging, open, and humane organizational culture." For guidelines on how to do so, see Phegan's book.

II

Developing Your Career

6

Essential Communication Skills

In all jobs planners take on, the ability to communicate effectively is essential, perhaps the most essential of all required skills. While they may seem rudimentary, communication skills will not diminish in importance as you advance in your career. If anything, the demand for sophisticated communication becomes greater as you move into higher positions, especially management ones. The key required communication skills are writing and editing; preparing graphics; making oral, written, and graphic presentations; giving clear directions and listening to others; and knowing how to respond to and manage the media.

"A leader has to be concerned with semantics."
—Martin Luther King, Jr.

PUTTING WORDS TOGETHER

First and foremost in your arsenal of skills must be the effective use of words. Whether in memos, e-mail messages, reports, technical studies, or oral presentations, the important thing is that messages, whatever they may be, are understood. This applies in both directions: not only must you assemble and use words with skill, you must also hear and understand the words of others.

The most fundamental word rules are:

- Use the active voice ("The cat scratched the boy" instead of "The boy was scratched by the cat.")

- Keep sentences short. And reports too, if possible, and certainly any summaries thereof.

- Use common, everyday words instead of obscure, multi-syllabic, academically chic words. Try hard, especially in public settings, not to use words like paradigm, parameter, dichotomy, systemic, normative, conurbation, econometric, prototypical, social overhead, interface, conceptualized, concretized, agendized, incrementalized, comprehensive problem-solving strategy, imageability, empirical, prioritize, and the like. All are perfectly good words or expressions except when you are trying to communicate with the general public, especially those who have not spent any time in academia and do not know, and do not want to learn, academic language.

- Make every sentence and paragraph clear and unambiguous.

- Talk and write in a persuasive manner. Remember that in many cases you are trying to sell ideas and should not shy away from finding inventive ways to do so.

- Get to the point, and quickly. If you can say what needs to be said in three minutes, don't take 15. If one page of text tells the story, or enough of the story, don't use five pages.

- Keep your eyes on the other person; if his or her eyes wander or glaze over, or the body language changes, you have lost him or her and need to regroup or conclude the conversation at once.

What you must avoid when using words and assembling sentences:

- Being cute or flippant (although employing humor is not forbidden in the right circumstances if you know how and when to do so);

- Being ponderous, pious, or long-winded;

- Preaching, lecturing, being condescending, or lording it over the people to whom you are making a presentation; and

- Using jargon that may work when talking with colleagues but is out of place elsewhere.

Spell-Check Programs and Other Dangers

By all means, run a spell-check program on your document after word processing is finished. Just don't let this step substitute for proofreading by an actual human. Almost all planners have made the mistake of typing "pubic" when they meant "public," and since both are legitimate words the spell-check program is not going to save you this embarrassment. Also avoid asking your computer to do a wholesale replacement of one word with another unless you are absolutely certain about the consequences. One planner did a global change to replace "table" with "figure" (the preferred term for graphics) and found that throughout the report chapter on schools the word "portable" had been changed to "porfigure." Your computer may be handy, but it is not smart (yet).

"Today's Tip for Writers: When writing a business report, avoid big words and jargon; try to use everyday language. Wrong: We will prioritize the infrastructure paradigm matrices. Right: We are fixin' to prioritize the infrastructure paradigm matrices."
—Dave Barry, newspaper columnist and humorist Santa Rosa (California) Press Democrat, June 27, 1999).

GIVING AND FOLLOWING DIRECTIONS

Because you may not be addressing the multitudes in your first few months on the job, the most important communication skill you will need at the outset is the ability to communicate with co-workers, including your immediate supervisor. At this point in the game, you probably will need to use your ears twice as much as your mouth. Can you really take directions? Do you listen all the way through? Do you ask questions about any details you don't understand, or do you grasp at what you think is the gist of what is said to you (and maybe get it wrong)?

If you find that the people you work with and for are often misunderstanding you and vice versa, then you need to work harder to reach understanding. You may also need to make sure the people instructing you are doing so thoroughly and accurately; if they are not, keep insisting that they try. Check on whether you both understand the content of the directions before leaving the subject. For example, when your supervisor gives you a task, summarize his or her request in your own words. Sometimes you have to try an interpretation that goes beyond what was said, because many people make no allowance for the gap between their experience (standard operating procedure) and yours (what's

"Everybody gets so much information all day long that they lose their common sense." —Gertrude Stein

going on here?). Bear in mind also that in some cases supervisors do not do much supervising, for any of several unfortunate reasons, in which case you may be on your own and required to figure out for yourself what to do next and even what is implied in the imperfect messages that you receive from your supervisor.

Also bear in mind that as time goes on you will have people reporting to you and over whom you will have supervisorial responsibilities. What is good for the goose is good for the gander, which is to say that those qualities that you admire in your supervisor or others of authority or influence ought to carry forward in your behavior as a manager, and those qualities that have little to commend them ought to be purged from your arsenal of management traits. (See further discussion in Chapter 7, "Essential Management Skills".)

COMMUNICATING UPWARD

Even more difficult is giving directions or passing on information, selling an idea or a proposal, or otherwise communicating something you know well to a person above you—a supervisor or a client—who knows little or nothing about the subject. When you are speaking to a supervisor, such as a chief administrative officer, CEO, or planning director, or to political figures, or to the public at large, you often run into James's Law of Ignorance, which states: "The time taken for a clever man to influence a stupid man is inversely proportional to the gap in their knowledge."

This is not to say that supervisors or politicians or the public are stupid, although a few will prove to you that they are. Rather, they may know and perceive less than you. In the context of reporting to others, or in attempting to persuade, the key ingredients here are diligence, perseverance, patience, and tact. In fact, they are the key ingredients under even the best of circumstances, even among associates and friendly and receptive audiences. Another ingredient is to be well prepared and thereby well equipped to pass along information, proposals, or requests with purpose, clarity, and certitude.

COMMUNICATING WITH THE PUBLIC

One skill rarely taught in schools is dealing with the public. Maybe your first job will be one in which you have to explain the rules of the game, perhaps certain local land use or building regulations, to someone who wants to do something that government regulates and for which some sort of permit is required. For many ordinary citizens, this is their big and maybe only face-to-face contact or confrontation with government. Let's hope you are equipped to represent the agency well, causing the citizen to leave your office with a grateful and positive attitude. What you want to avoid is making a lasting negative impression on some innocent taxpayer, which can add to the widely held feeling that government people are unresponsive and hard to deal with without an attorney to smooth the way. You want to prove the very opposite—and ought to strive to do that every day.

Another form of working and communicating with the public takes place during the plan-making process, in which citizens participate (through citizens advisory committees) in assisting and directing professionals. This subject is dealt with in depth in Chapter 8, "Essential Political Skills."

The main overriding guidelines for communicating with the public are:

- Be cooperative and helpful as you attempt to communicate the rules, regulations and procedures that govern what people can do or how a planning process really works. It is best to make things as simple and straightforward for the public as possible, even if you're not the least bit responsible for creating the system you have to work with.

- Be direct and honest even when you are conveying a message that people don't want to hear. Be tactful, but don't sugar-coat to make people feel good.

- Do not engage in evasions and put-downs. People may not know the rules or regulations as you do, or the jargon of your job, or the process of plan-making; these are not reasons to treat them with disrespect. Public employees and consultants often must be educators so that communication can take place properly. Being an effective educator means knowing how to exercise patience and a helping hand.

- Do not maintain a social distance that is bound to evoke resentments. Examples of such snobby behavior include using difficult or uncommon terms or being outwardly amused and unhelpful when asked a "simplistic" question. Some planners do this in a smart-aleck fashion because of some need to lord over the public. Or, maybe (worse yet) they show signs of not wanting to mix it up with people of a different socioeconomic class or level of education. It is unseemly and counterproductive to be that way.

PRESENTING YOURSELF IN PUBLIC

Whether you are a public agency planner, a consultant, a real estate developer, or a nonprofit representative, you may have to venture out in public and communicate what your work is all about to people whom you want to inform or persuade. There is the danger that you will antagonize, confuse, load down with too much information, bore, or fail to persuade your audience. It is much more likely that, with considerable experience and some guidelines in mind, you will learn to take command of meetings and cause your audience to give your presentations their rapt attention.

Here are a few things to keep in mind when making a presentation:

- Don't just show up, show up prepared. Know what your subject is all about and what you are doing with it. Wear an appropriate "costume." A three-piece suit may be fine if your client is the CEO of Bank of America but would be completely out of place in any rural community. Be sure there's an agenda. If you are bringing along visual aids, set them up before the chairperson convenes the meeting. Post any wall-sized graphics prominently so that attendees can examine them before the meeting begins and during or after presentations.

- Know what you want to get from your presentation. Identify your audience and what the optimum response would be. Do you simply want to impart information? Do you want to offer advice and recommendations? Do you want to get approval of a proposal? Do you want directions on what to do next?

- Make sure your presentation allows time for discussion and feedback, and that you are prepared to handle questions and criticisms.

- Make sure the timing of your presentation is correct and optimum. Is it coming in the proper stage in the decision process, and does your audience understand that process and the purpose of the meeting?

- Identify the highlights and focus on them. If you control the meeting, do not let audience members run off on tangents.

- Don't distribute printed materials just before you're going to speak lest your audience becomes too busy reading to listen and participate. On the other hand, there is rarely a case when written materials and graphic displays are an ill-considered part of any presentation, so be sure you have your materials ready for timely distribution and display, depending on the situation.

- Learn how to listen to what people are saying. This includes listening for the obvious, but also for hidden or disguised feelings, hidden agendas, and political posturing. For example, people resisting assisted housing in their neighborhood may be talking about how damaging to property values cheaper (assisted) housing would be, when they really mean that they are afraid of having people in their neighborhood who accept welfare payments and food stamps.

- Don't be defensive or evasive when hard questions are asked. It won't hurt to say, "I don't know, but if you want me to, I'll find out and report back."

- Remember that meetings are often a form of theater as well as purposeful events. Learn to judge how best to engage your audience and how to act your part. Being relaxed and even a tad amusing or witty is not a bad idea, even if the subject matter is serious.

- Keep a record of public comments, through use of video, audio recordings, butcher-paper notes, or minutes. Offer to provide copies of the record.

A WORD ABOUT GRAPHICS AND VISUAL DISPLAYS

Getting your message across either in written or oral presentations may require the use of maps, charts, tables, slides, videos, architectural renderings, and other project-appropriate graphics. You may be responsible for putting these together yourself (and you might be quite good at it), or you may require help. Either way, a few points to keep in mind:

- Keep it simple. Most graphics and visual displays can only convey one (or at the most two) messages clearly, although maps can be the exception. Think about that you want each graphic to "say."

- Plan your graphics to fit the circumstances. A report graphic may not be effective as a wall graphic at a meeting, and vice versa.

- Remember your audience. While you are probably very comfortable with data presented in tables or charts, for example, many people—including some very well-educated people—are completely flummoxed at the sight of a table or chart. It is usually best to explain the data with words too. If the information is especially important, see if you can communicate it in various different ways—through words, in a table, and on a map, for example—so that you will be getting through to as many people as possible.

- Make sure that reports include the most crucial maps and graphics, even if they have to be reduced in size from wall maps or graphs, or condensed for report-size use. People want to have reference points within a report, and since most will be taking your report home for further study it is vitally important that they have all of the useful graphics available to them for reference purposes.

- Do not hesitate to include photographs in reports or employ slides or other visual aids at public meetings—not as fillers but as substantive contributions to getting a message across.

WORKING WITH THE MEDIA

For the newly appointed, no task can be more daunting or full of mine fields than trying to communicate with and manage the media. In most cases they will be in attendance at public hearings and will pick up what is presented. This is not to say, however, that they necessarily will report on your presentation and the audience reactions to it as you would hope. Remember, what you say is likely to be printed in the next issue of the local newspaper, so be sure to highlight what you want to see printed and avoid saying anything that if printed will embarrass you, your boss, or your client, or misrepresent the realities of the situation.

Often it is prudent to write and issue press releases to the media. Doing this may serve your interest as well as cause your findings or recommendations to be properly quoted or characterized. Getting to know the reporter is not a bad idea, since this often facilitates understanding of and communication about the essence of your project; but even then it is always wise to avoid saying anything that you do not want to appear in print, because that is exactly what will happen if it is printable, especially if it is controversial, radical, or otherwise "newsworthy" as defined by reporters or television interviewers. (See more discussion of media handling in Chapter 8, "Essential Political Skills.")

CHAPTER

7

Essential Management Skills

The term "manager" refers to "one who conducts business affairs with economy and care." In most planning-related jobs, demanding work and tight budgets make being a manager a tricky balancing act, even if you're only managing yourself. This chapter outlines some of the skills necessary to being a good manager of yourself and others.

An important observation: The demand for competent managers in the planning field has always been strong, and is growing stronger. As new technology develops and regulations become ever more complex, the need for people who can oversee a project and shepherd it through to completion is increasing. Planners, trained as generalists, are often uniquely equipped for this role. If you have any innate management and leadership skills, you should certainly nurture and develop them. In that light, the general guidelines offered in this chapter are no substitute for a study of the many styles of management and related topics essential to a full understanding of effective managing. If this subject interests you, consult the literature or consider enrolling in the many management courses offered by local colleges, universities, and other groups.

MAKING DECISIONS

Anyone who allocates resources or time, offers advice, or implements policy is an executive. All executives face the problem of making the right decisions on what they themselves or others should do. Many people think that decisions are always made at the top. Not so—everyone in the workplace makes decisions, because not all decisions are big ones, and some are delegated by a higher authority. For example, an entry-level planner in a public agency may need to decide what to do about regulating and penalizing the owners of housing built without permits (subject, of course, to prevailing rules, regulations, and restraints on abuse of power).

Using that example, here are some steps for making decisions that tap your best judgmental powers:

1. *Do your homework first.* Do you have all or enough of the facts? What principle or rule should your decision establish? Do you want to have all illegal houses decriminalized, penalized, or merely forced to be brought up to code?

2. *Know your decision-making style.* Do you believe in making decisions based strictly on the facts? Based on political trends? Based on personal values and perceptions? Your decision-making style may rely mainly on one of these factors, or combine all of them. Regardless, if your style differs from others, be patient and flexible. Try to understand the points of view of other managers, policymakers, and co-workers, even when their styles are hard to comprehend.

3. *Identify the limits of the decision.* Do you want the rule to apply only to whole structures or to illegal additions as well? Will new violators be treated the same as pre-decision violators? Who will be involved in the impacts of your decision? How will they be affected?

4. *Think first about what is right and what will achieve the best results.* Leave compromises, concessions, and political assessments for later on. Thus, you may decide that the best result for regulating illegal residences is not to punish the owners per se, but to require them to rent to low-income residents after bringing the units up to code.

5. *Develop the means to implement your decision.* Illegal homes, for example, could be brought up to code by using low-interest housing rehabilitation loans. This would actually improve the value of the owner's property and make the action more acceptable. That's the carrot. The stick could be the code authority to fine or to order the work done when owners do not comply.

6. *Circulate the decision to other knowledgeable people and stakeholders.* Evaluate their comments and prepare some options and fallback positions. Be sure your tactics for gaining

approval have some feasible alternatives. This requires a strategy that is flexible enough to allow the decision to emerge from the political process reshaped but unbroken.

7. *Monitor progress and evaluate results.* Once the decision is made and actions are being carried out, monitor the situation to see how well things are working. Is the system that was finally adopted solving the illegal housing problem the way you thought it would? If not, what improvements could be made?

Attributes of Managers, Directors, and CEOs

Although you may have a long way to go before you reach a top position in an agency or firm, it's worth being aware of what's in store for you should you elect to take on such an assignment one day. To that end, and only briefly, here are some attributes one needs for a lead position.

Whether you're a director of an agency, a city or county manager, leader of a nonprofit group, or chief executive officer (CEO) of a private-sector firm, the required attributes and skills are pretty much the same. They include:

- Being prepared to be the ultimate decision-maker in the organization.

- Being strong-willed and energetic.

- Being able to guide, encourage, support, and motivate all those working for you, listen to and convey respect for them, and foster a creative working environment.

- Having budgeting and money-management skills, and the self-discipline to guide and control all aspects of expenditures and all persons connected with money-handling.

- Knowing all there is to know about personnel management and rules, including, if relevant, relationships with union representatives.

- Being good at managing advisory committees, legislative bodies, boards of directors—and if appropriate steering them to accomplish what you think best for the agency, firm, or community.

- Knowing more about the organization and the community in which it functions than anyone else, including those on any overseeing commission, council, or board. (You should be able to amaze people with your detailed knowledge of the organization, its history, and its policies and programs.)

- Being able to deal with the agency's, company's, or community's movers and shakers—as a virtual equal.

- Being able, when necessary, to usher erring employees to the door quickly and quietly, subject, of course, to fair employment practices, policies, or acts.

In addition, effective managers know that no single person in any organization has enough eyes, ears, or smarts to see everything that's going on. You need good people around you with whom you can share ideas, and sometimes even power. These people may include an associate (assistant director), or someone on your board of directors or legislative body. But, while sharing ideas and even some power may work for you, you must maintain authority and have an ability to make decisions. If you fear the political consequences of making decisions, and determine that making no decision is the safest course, then you are not doing the job you were hired to do, and in the process you will be letting others down. When you hand over some decision-making power (i.e., delegate authority) to someone else, for good reasons or bad, you are still accountable for what happens. In the end, having the right kind of people in your organization is what counts.

KEEPING TRACK OF BUDGETS

No matter where you work, you will almost always face the question of "where will the money come from?" Unlike in school, projects in the workplace are governed by the amount of money available. And it's likely that most of the money in your workplace will be spent on staff people's time, not on other, more tangible items such as supplies. This means that sometimes you won't be able to spend as much time (i.e., money) on a project as you would like. But having a budget can also have its advantages, by helping you to set priorities for your work tasks and schedule your time. The amount of money and time available can help you to determine which aspects of your project need to be done right, no matter what, and which ones may have to slide a little. Keeping track of the budget can also alert you to when your project is in trouble—for example, you have spent most of the money and are nowhere close to submitting a product or achieving a result.

Unlike in school, in the workplace "time equals money."

As you begin your career, you may not ultimately be responsible for the budgets of the projects you work on, or the budget for your office as a whole. Nonetheless, whoever is overseeing the budget will appreciate your efforts to monitor and stay within the budget, and to identify projects or tasks that should be cut or added to the budget.

Nonprofit and Private-Sector Budgets

In the private sector, the age-old truth is that "time equals money." Here's how it works in a consulting firm, for example: A client agrees to pay your firm some amount of money, in exchange for some sort of product. Your firm agrees to the budget amount, probably based on an estimate of the time and expenses involved in producing whatever it is the client wants. The firm translates the time estimate into a budget by determining the number of hours each firm member will spend on the project and assigning each member an hourly billing rate (see sidebar, "How You Fit Into Your Firm's Budget" on page 103). Each person's billing rate includes his/her salary and benefits, as well as general expenses associated with having that person in the office—rent for the office space, utilities, and so on. If the project ends up taking much more time than originally estimated, the firm will begin to lose money. For this reason, you will want to keep careful records of the amount of time you spend on the project, and on what tasks, so that the firm can make sure that it is doing what it said it would do (and not too much more) within the agreed-upon budget.

In other types of private businesses, such as real estate and housing development companies, the money may come from different sources, such as bank loans. The basic idea remains the same, however: The company allocates the total project budget among the various tasks involved in getting the project done (a new hotel built, for example). You will need to complete your part of the work within a set budget. If too many different work tasks take more time and money than expected, the project will be in danger and the hotel may never be built.

Nonprofit organizations manage budgets in much the same way. The funding for nonprofit work often comes from foundations and other benevolent organizations, rather than from private clients or institutions. Even though the source of the money is slightly different from private-sector sources, the basic relationship is much the same: The nonprofit has proposed a project, and the foundation has agreed to fund it. This relationship is often established through a grant program, in which the nonprofit submits a proposal to accomplish a project that the foundation is interested in. Once the foundation provides the grant money, it will want to see that the project is moving forward as the nonprofit originally promised. This usually means that the nonprofit will submit quarterly reports or some other written documentation of the amount of time used, the work performed, and progress toward completing the project. Again, you will want to keep careful track of the time you have spent, the tasks you have completed, and the milestones you have achieved.

You may discover along the way that funds are insufficient to accomplish project objectives without additional staff help. This is often the case, resulting in staff working longer hours than planned and/or the project being delayed. A clever manager might recruit unpaid volunteers to help out. It is rarely good form to go back to the client, governing board, or other funding source to ask for more money. (An exception might involve a client that has asked you to complete work that wasn't included in your original agreement.)

How You Fit Into Your Firm's Budget

Suppose that the consulting firm you work for pays you, Associate Planner A, at the wage rate of $40 per hour. The firm "marks up" this amount by 1.5 to 3 times (depending on the firm) to cover the firm's operating expenses, overhead, and profit. (Public-sector agencies have their own ways of valuing the worth of their employees, which is at least the sum of the wages paid and employee benefits promised.) In this manner, the firm applies a cost per hour to each employee.

Accordingly, if the firm lands a project that will require 10 weeks (or 400 hours) of your time, the firm will bill the client a total of $48,000 for Associate Planner A's time, assuming a "mark-up" of 3.0 ($40 per hour x 3.0 = $120 per hour x 400 hours = $48,000). The firm will also add other expenses, such as maps, photos, and travel, to the bill.

If you, Associate Planner A, are efficient, and nothing goes wrong, the firm will realize its full margin of expected operating expense income, overhead income, and profit. If not, the extra hours worked by Associate Planner A to complete the project will eat into the margin (i.e., the difference between all direct costs and the billable fee)—and make your employer unhappy (and unable to buy the family yacht). A good manager will not allow this latter scenario to happen, and an inefficient employee will soon be job hunting.

Public Sector Budgets

The public sector, too, increasingly manages employees' time according to the amount of money available. Public agencies are funded by federal, state, and local taxes, and (in most cases) fees charged for services. Traditionally, agencies have managed this money by developing "line-item budgets," which list an amount to be spent on each staff position, supplies, and other expenses, usually on an annual basis. Increasingly, though, public agencies are switching to "program budgets" to encourage efficient use of time and to shift the agency's focus onto products and results. A program budget assigns funding by program (or project), rather than by line item; this allows the agency to keep closer track of how each employee's time is actually used for each project.

Using program budgets, public agencies may function like private-sector offices, but not always. (When they don't, it's because of poor oversight and/or the absence of any penalties for failure to balance a budget, or because "losses" can be carried over into the next fiscal year.) Each project receives a budget, and the project manager is responsible for making sure that the project is completed within budget. The project may have its own "line-item budget"; the project manager may list the amount of money assigned to each staff person's time, supplies, expenses, travel, and so on. The program budget approach essentially passes along these "line-item" budgeting responsibilities to the person actually in charge of the project, i.e., the project manager.

Some aspects of public-sector budgets differ from those of other workplaces. For example, a local planning department's budget will usually assign some amount of money to "current planning" (i.e., processing development applications, environmental impact reports, etc.). Current planning work differs from other "programs" or "projects"; the department may have no idea how many applications it will receive during any given year, and thus estimating workload and budget needs becomes very difficult. Past history is typically used to generate some sort of estimate. Thus, if you work in current planning, keeping track of your time becomes all the more important. If you begin receiving many more applications than expected, your department might hire a planner on a temporary, often contract basis, using funding from the windfall of application fees. Some public agencies have begun using "cost recovery" programs (i.e., charging applicants for the full cost of processing development and environmental review applications) to address these uncertainties in current planning budgets.

MANAGING YOUR (AND OTHER PEOPLE'S) TIME

Developing Work Programs

To complete most projects at your workplace, you will probably need to decide who will do what, and by when. Planners have a term for this: "developing a work program." For small, relatively simple projects with few people involved, you may not need a formal, written work program. More complicated, long-term projects usually demand some kind of work program, whether it's a written description or a calendar or matrix with the participants' time blocked out on it and key milestones noted. Here are four possible ways of drafting a simple work program for a one-month-long project involving you (Dreyfus) and your boss (Ms. Ace Goodman). These are examples only (and relatively simple ones at that). Your organization may have its own work program format, or you may develop your own based on the nature of the job and the number of people/entities involved. (In fact, you should learn to do so.)

Option One

This work program highlights the target dates for each action.

Scheduled Date	Action
August 2-13	Dreyfus prepares draft report
August 16	Dreyfus submits draft report to Goodman for review
August 16-20	Goodman reviews draft report
August 23	Goodman returns report to Dreyfus for revisions
August 23-27	Dreyfus revises draft report
August 30	Dreyfus submits final report to client

Option Two

This option adds billing information for each task. Consultants not only create work programs similar to this simple example, but also record person hours and monitor whether the staff is meeting the scheduled dates and staying within the project budget.

Scheduled Date	Action	Person Hours	Billable Rate Per Hour	Amount to be Charged to Client
Aug 2-13	Dreyfus prepares draft	30	$100	$3,000
Aug 16	Dreyfus submits draft to Goodman	—	—	—
Aug 16-20	Goodman reviews draft	5	$150	$750
Aug 23	Goodman returns report to Dreyfus for revisions	—	—	—
Aug 23-27	Dreyfus revises report	10	$100	$1,000
Aug 30	Dreyfus submits final report to client	2	$100	$200

Option Three

This work program highlights the actions and which staff member is responsible carrying them out.

Action	Responsible Staff/Scheduled Dates	
	Dreyfus	Goodman
Draft report prepared	August 2-13	---
Draft report submitted for review	August 16	---
Draft report reviewed	---	August 16-20
Draft report returned for revisions	---	August 23
Draft report revised	August 23-27	---
Final report submitted to client	August 30	

Option Four

This work program shows the same information in a graph, rather than table, form.

Responsible Staff:		
Goodman	☐	Reviews draft report
Dreyfus		
Prepares/submits draft report		Revises draft report
☐		☐
		FINAL REPORT SUBMITTED TO CLIENT ☐

1.2.3.4.5.6.7.8.9.10.11.12.13.14.15.16.17.18.19.20.21.22.23.24.25.26.27.28.29.30.31
August

To develop a work program, you will need to identify work tasks and juggle people's schedules to ensure that your project gets done on time. Here is a checklist of items you will want to consider.

What is the final product going to be? A report? If so, what will it contain? Recommendations, research findings, a summary or abstract (almost always a good idea), maps, graphs, tables, and so on? Is the documentation and source material going to be published in the report or in a separate document?

How will you tell your story when the product is finished? This is the time to think about any public presentation materials that you'll want to illustrate your main points—and who will prepare them.

How and to whom will you distribute your product? Who is the audience? The public? Policymakers? The media? Thinking about this will help you to budget your time and identify the full range of products you will be preparing. Consider what your audience is likely to read. Most people don't like to read fat reports; they would rather have some kind of summary. The media might prefer a press release, rather than a copy of the report itself; most reporters, left to their own devices, would rather report on a conflict than on the contents or merits of a planning program.

If the budget allows, an inexpensive tabloid edition for the public with a mail-back form for reaction may be a good option. Policymakers and other key players can get a full, glossy copy with a summary, while other technicians, organizations, archives, and libraries can receive a photocopy with a supplement that describes the supporting research methods, statistics, data sources, and other documentation.

Consider whether you will need discussion drafts of the document you are preparing. In a public process, these drafts can be a very good idea politically, as well as technically, because they allow you to incorporate corrections and important revisions suggested by participants in the process. Discussion drafts are also good as trial balloons for policy or program recommendations, to get debate going and discover the nature of the opposition while fallback positions are still possible. Recommendations that surface later usually have less chance of surviving the political process, because the talking and negotiating stage has been bypassed and someone's interest must lose in order for the other to win. This is a situation that politicians abhor. By issuing discussion drafts, you deal with possible controversy at the outset and decrease the chance that conflict later on will derail your project.

What data do you need? If you have existing information to work with, is it of good quality? Is it current, or obsolete? Once you know this, you can set the level of precision at which you're going to have to work. If new information is needed, be sure you know how much it's going to cost to get it, and decide whether it's worth the cost. If there's still uncertainty (and there usually is), then determine how much pursuit of more data you're going to allow. Some data-compilation addicts love to immerse themselves in a sea of statistics without restraints on when they have to surface and be reviewed for significant results.

Who is going to do the work? Will the project team include people in your office, other agencies' staff, consultants? Temporary inexperienced people, or full-time experienced staff? Know who's going to be able to do what, when. In many organizations (especially bureaucratic ones), new work has a hard time fitting in, because standard operating procedures ensure that regular work will expand to fill the time available. How is the work going to be coordinated if it has to flow among people in different departments, consultants, citizen advisory groups, and so on? Very often you will have the responsibility for getting work out of various sovereign entities, when your authority doesn't extend beyond the power to plead. One good way to be sure that work assignments are clearly understood is to distribute preliminary and final drafts of the work program to everyone involved.

What is the schedule? How fast is the product or any part of it really needed? The best technique, once you've got a fixed date, is to construct a calendar that begins with that date and works backward to the date the work starts. Then systematically lay out the number of weeks required for each task and work rigorously to get each task done on time. (In school, you, like most of us, may have learned to ignore or play games with this sort of reality and to put production off until the last moment. Incontrovertibly, this habit must be unlearned quickly and replaced with a workable schedule. Last-minute cramming in the workplace is out of the question!) Make sure that the schedule allows for internal reviews and public participation as necessary. By doing this, you and everyone else involved can recognize that, while you may commit to firm deadlines for delivering your products, others over whom you have no control may cause delays.

Are there important external events that may change the fate of the project? (Examples include an election that may remove supporters from office, or a grant for a three-year project only funded on a year-to-year basis.) Sometimes it may be good to stretch projects out so that they can reach logical cutoff points before completion. Do not use too large a budget in any one year if it will make the project a political target. Stretching out the work also may let the program results emerge after enemies are out of office. (This is called "letting the dinosaurs die off," i.e., bypassing the people who are likely to vote "no" or avoid a decision by sending the matter back for "more study.")

Being a Project Manager

If the work program assigns you to oversee the team's work and to ensure that the product is completed, then you are the project manager—even if ultimately you will submit the product to your own boss for approval. Being a manager means depending on others to produce work you're responsible for sending out as finished. You will be putting out fires and running interference that other team members cannot handle, as well as reviewing the team's work. (If working this way does not suit your personality, avoid promotions to management jobs.)

Being a manager means depending on others to produce work you're responsible for sending out in finished form.

When you are the one in charge of seeing that work gets done, then "seeing" becomes part of your job. Periodically (every day or every week, depending on tightness of schedule), check in with the other people on the project and discuss their work. Do not feel reluctant to "bird dog" a task—this is part of your job as manager. Cover at least these two questions:

- **"What have you accomplished since we last talked?"** This establishes what progress has been made, and whether you and the other person have the same understanding of what's supposed to be produced, and when. Directions that you thought were perfectly clear may have been misunderstood, and it's vital to get things back on track before too much detouring has occurred. Some people can't stay on track very long before they go spinning off on a tangent. This can be particularly true of bright, creative people (often generalists with no management experience but with lots of good ideas and good intentions) who like to improvise, rather than "cook by the book." It's important to make sure that all team members understand how and why their pieces fit into the bigger picture. Always listen, and be open to fresh ideas from people who are doing the work. Don't be a know-it-all who only issues commands. Try to be a coordinator or facilitator, rather than a supervisor. Sometimes this means you work for someone who is under you on the organization chart to remove obstacles, resolve delays and priority conflicts, and get things done.

- *"When are you going to finish?"* When you ask this question, it's important to remember that there's a fine line between nagging and taking a continuing interest in someone's work. People rarely have only your project to work on, and even more rarely do they have complete control over their time. If someone is getting bogged down because they're getting conflicting demands, get the conflict settled immediately with the person caught in the crossfire and with the others involved if necessary. Only the individuals doing the work know what their work pace is and what their obligations to other projects are. You need to negotiate for completion dates and get a commitment for such deadlines. Set a target date when the task is assigned, and then revise it if necessary for good and defensible reasons.

Another important note: Completing the work means presenting answers, not questions, to the person who reviews the work. The junior person should take responsibility for writing so that the senior person will be able to concentrate on the content rather than being diverted by the need to correct spelling, grammar, sentence structure, and composition. Completed work is something a senior person could feel confident in signing, rather than editing and reworking. Rough drafts are not precluded, but they should not be half-baked excuses for shifting the work up to the senior level.

Once you receive the team's work, you will need to review it. Consider whether you feel comfortable staking your professional reputation on the reception this work would receive when it leaves your desk or your office. If you would not, ask tough questions of the authors until you're satisfied that any inconsistencies or errors have been combed out, and that the work is ready for review and criticism on questions of policy, rather than quality. Make sure the team gets to review your work in the same light.

"By working faithfully eight hours a day, you may eventually get to be a boss and work 12 hours a day." —Robert Frost (1875-1963), American poet

Handling Foul-Ups

Sometimes things just don't go as planned. You, or others working with you or for you, occasionally might make a bad decision,
an error in judgment, or a technical mistake. Some tips for handling these sometimes difficult circumstances:

- Don't cover up. Discuss the foul-ups openly and take responsibility for what happened.

- Don't stay with things that clearly aren't working. Cut away
  fast and go on to something else.

- Negotiate for lower expectations. For example, the computer
  mapping system turns out unusable mush. Back to the draw-
  ing board, then, and make do with paper maps until a new
  system can be developed.

- Don't embarrass others by pointing fingers at them (even
  when they are the ones at fault). Try to work together to solve
  the problem. This will do wonders for maintaining morale.

- Even if the people you have to work with aren't what you really want or need, remember it's usually better to have some
  kind of help rather than do all the work yourself.

- Accept your losses and try to learn from them. Don't try to
  recapture them by cutting corners or cheating on the rest of the
  project. The value of the results will suffer, and you'll risk a
  bigger failure. Make sure you won't be caught by the same
  mistakes again.

- Remember that you haven't failed if you tried your best and
  your project recommendations weren't understood or accepted. Don't try to own the problem, just because you started
  working on it first. Think of all the people in history whose
  truth was ahead of its time. Try to substitute a philosophical
  (or Zen) attitude for frustration.

Managing Time Spent in Meetings

Meetings are an inevitable part of work life, but they can be un-
productive time-wasters if they are not managed properly. Many
meetings are too long, often by twice. While some people genuinely enjoy meetings (perhaps as time away from other responsibilities, or as time fillers), for most professionals and otherwise
busy people the lost time can be frustrating. It will prove to be so

for you too unless you (a) are equipped with a pillow, (b) bring something to read or to knit, or (c) can grab hold of the meeting and move it along.

Managing meetings and their duration is a learned skill and is worth the effort. While no one should be prevented from participating, a good chairperson will limit redundancies and motor mouths, and will be disciplined and firm enough to manage meeting time and loquacious talkers.

You may not be in charge of all, or even any, of the meetings you attend, but you can still try to make a meeting as productive as possible through your own conduct there. All attendees, not just the chairperson, should be prepared for a meeting and mindful of moving things along.

"Meetings are indispensable when you don't want to do anything." — John Kenneth Galbraith, Harvard professor emeritus, author, and former ambassador to India

Staff Meetings. Meetings among people in your office, whether a project team meeting or an office-wide staff meeting, have two possible purposes:

- To make sure everyone gets the same information simultaneously and that everyone understands the message; and/or

- To put ideas and finished work up for review by the project team or office. This is an opportunity to test the work as a whole before informed but critical colleagues who can identify any major flaws. It is also an opportunity to bestow recognition on people who have done important work, but who won't share the public limelight.

Keep these purposes in mind in conducting yourself at these meetings, or in conducting the meeting as a whole if you are in charge. If there will be many points to cover during the meeting, make an agenda (or offer to make one if you are not in charge). During the meeting, make your contributions brief and to-the-point; avoid long explanations that people don't really need to hear. If you are the chairperson of the meeting, try to cut monologues short as tactfully as possible (including your own!). Also avoid conversations that involve only two co-workers but that several others are forced to listen to. These waste people's time; schedule a separate meeting with the key people instead. At the end of the meeting, make sure everyone knows what they have agreed to do, and by when. If you sense that people haven't understood their assignments, feel free to speak up, even if you aren't in charge of the meeting.

Other Meetings. Meetings with others—clients, consultants, citizens advisory committees, policymakers, other agency staff, grant givers, and so on—should be scheduled only when:

- A decision needs to be made (for example, more money is needed to complete a project).

- There is a need to sort out possible misunderstandings.

- Information needs to be exchanged, and it cannot be done accurately or efficiently by means other than a face-to-face meeting.

The same rules that govern internal office meetings also apply here. Try to keep the discussion brief and on-point, and make sure everyone understands their marching orders at the end of the meeting.

MANAGING PAPERWORK

Paperwork will be a fact of life at your workplace. But paper doesn't have to swamp you.

Pushing Paper

Some tips for managing the daily deluge of paper in your office:

- Delegate authority to send notes, memos, and letters to anyone who can write intelligently. Don't be one of those channels everything in writing must go through.

- If you're asked to review something, don't nit-pick. Write briefly in the margins, rather than composing a memo or book report as you did in school. If possible, suggest alternative language rather than just noting a problem or making a comment.

- Send correspondence and copies only to those with a valid need to know.

Writing Reports

Reports may be the main products of your office. If so, there can be a temptation to make them as fat as possible. Consider whether every project you work on needs to be memorialized by a big, thick report. Why not try a skinny one, backed by a fat file, from which copies can be sent to the people who really need all that information?

Most organizations have a standard report format for all to follow. That's not to say that you cannot recommend changes. A good report usually has the following characteristics:

- *A short title* that explains the purpose of the report.

- *A summary or abstract* that describes the results of your work. This is the place for any recommendations.

- *An introduction* that states as clearly and simply as possible what the report is about.

- *A main text* that takes the reader through the reasoning of the report in logical steps. (Try not to detour through the history of the subject, minutia about methodology used, and long tables showing the data analyzed.)

- *A conclusion* (and perhaps an action program) that summarizes what should be done, why, and by whom.

- *Appendices and exhibits* only as necessary. (These report fatteners should be bound into the report for general distribution only if there is a compelling reason to do so.)

- A list of *credits and sources.*

Writing Memos

Memos are the tools of coordination and protection in most agencies. As such, they should be clear and concise, and state the response or action needed from the recipients.

As coordinating tools, memos can inform others about something or solicit a response, usually by describing one or more of the following:

- How to do something or why something needs to be done.

- What was done when and with whom.

- How to check out things before going ahead.

- Why changes should be or were made to something.

- What can be done now that we are running out of money, time, or supplies for a project.

- Additional facts that were forgotten earlier but that you now think need more explanation.

Memos can also serve as "protection." They can document who agreed to what, when, and why, and get others to share responsibility, thereby helping you and your organization to avoid trouble later on. To this end, you can use memos in the following ways:

- To note what was said at a meeting, and to justify an action for which you may be held accountable. An example would be a memo documenting a conversation with a citizen or client who calls with a complaint. Your memo says you will look into the matter and report back on what can be done. However, the citizen or client later gripes to your boss that you promised to solve the problem immediately. Your memo serves as documentation of your verbal agreement. (It's usually a good idea to send these difficult people copies of memos documenting conversations with them.)

- To document the position, facts, sources, and so on, on a topic you will probably get back to later on.

- To note that you were authorized, ordered, or directed to do something by higher-ups.

Using E-Mail

E-mail is handy for day-to-day communication, and for requesting and receiving information quickly and efficiently. There are some pitfalls to this more casual form of communication, though. An e-mail message that you dash off at your computer and send without reviewing might contain errors or unfortunate wording that the recipient will misconstrue. This can have repercussions in some situations, since e-mail is an "of-record" form of communication and can even be subpoenaed where there is sufficient cause to do so (as can other forms of written communications). To avoid being the cause of headaches, ruffled feathers, and other (even more serious) problems, read each e-mail message you compose at least once before sending it. And be sure it is appropriate to send it at all given house rules and the politics of the situation.

In delicate situations, or when you want to keep a careful record of your communications, send a memo instead of (or in addition to) an e-mail message. There are two reasons for this. First, when you write something on paper, there's a better chance that you will let it sit on your desk for a bit, review it, and then catch a mistake or rough wording that you can fix. Secondly, paper communications are more formal and carry slightly more weight than electronic ones—something to consider if you anticipate political, legal, or other trouble.

Another important note: Try to avoid sending and receiving personal e-mail at work. E-mail is not private (though many think it is); it is not necessarily erasable and may therefore be used against you. Many workplaces are cracking down on the use of office time and equipment for personal chats via e-mail. And even if your boss doesn't mind, you may not want your personal life immortalized in the office computer system.

Handling Junk

In any office, the condition of files, records, and maps may be terrific, up-to-date, and readily useable—or may not be. Do not be surprised either way. Sometimes when paperwork sits around, you and your co-workers will forget why you're keeping it, or even develop a sentimental attachment to it. To combat this tendency, the following items should usually be thrown away before they take up permanent residence and clutter files forever:

- Rough drafts, sketches, handwritten notes and calculations, and other materials that went into studies and reports long since completed or never completed.

- Extra copies of notices, letters, memos, staff reports, and agendas.

- Correspondence, forms, minutes, and documents relating to projects abandoned, denied, never started, or closed out years ago.

Before you start tossing things, check whether your office has a policy on records management. (If not, consider helping to develop one.) Keep in mind, too, that you may need to hold onto certain items for legal or tax purposes. For example, your office may be legally required to keep some documents on file as part of a public record, or as part of a paper trail for a lawsuit. This can be especially important when the law requires that administrative steps and proper procedures be followed before a court will accept a case for adjudication. Once you know what the rules are, be rigorous about throwing things away (or thinning out files and putting them in storage) when they are no longer needed.

8

Essential Political Skills

Planning is a helping, policy-recommending, plan-making, and design profession, as well as a professional approach to initiating action and getting things done. It is a profession occupied by people trained to exercise defined skills and good judgment. It is often described as a sober, objective, and highly technical process. Less often does one hear or read—especially when one is still in college—that the skilled planner is often subject to or engaged in political activities within politicized settings and, at times, is him or herself a political figure or one of the actors in a political drama.

To be sure, some jobs in planning are strictly technical and are carried out backstage, where one need not know much about politics and the exercise of political power. But most planning jobs involve dealing with people appointed or elected to positions of political power or with citizens or citizen groups. Planning, more often than not, is a public decision-making process, and this means that, when all is said and done, planning is politics.

It becomes essential for planners, no matter the venue, to learn the following: the rules of the games citizens and political figures play; how both groups exercise their rightful powers; how planners can take lead roles in orchestrating citizen participation in policy- and plan-making; and how to deal with the collision of forces that is called politics, as well as to function in politically charged settings.

In this chapter, we first discuss how citizen power is exercised by citizens, and how planners and others deal with citizen power as well as mobilize citizens to help accomplish individual, organizational, or community goals. Second, we address the realities of political power as exercised by political figures and persons clearly identifiable as politicians. Finally, we suggest some guidelines for honing your own advocacy, lobbying, and political skills.

"The health of a democratic society may be measured by the quality of functions performed by private citizens."
—*Alexis de Tocqueville (1805-1859), author of* Democracy in America

WORKING WITH CITIZENS

That people have learned a lot in the last 30 years about how to protect the places they love, develop or preserve land and other resources, and accomplish other goals, is one of the significant stories of our times. People accomplish their goals through the expression of citizen power. Some citizens exercise their power by organizing to protest a proposed public or private action. Citizens may attempt to halt proposals that are perceived as potentially harmful environmentally, socially, or economically— such as a highway through a stable residential area, or the filling of a wetland for an auto mall. Objections may arise to the introduction of housing for low-income families into a middle-class suburb or a public agency's willingness to grant a permit for a billiard parlor in the face of neighborhood objections. These are essentially defensive engagements and may be considered meritorious and righteous by some, or ill-considered, classist, racist, or exclusionary by others.

On the other hand, a public agency may be engaged in creative and positive plan-making in search of solutions to urban deterioration, or in favor of managed growth, or in support of affordable housing projects or child care services, or to preserve open space resources. Here, citizens can be depended on to have points of view, a need to participate in the process, and their own unique ways of exercising their ultimate influence and power.

The topics addressed here under the broad umbrella of essential political skills required to deal with citizens and citizen groups include:

- Serving the needs of citizens who need information, assistance, permits, or guidance on how to comply with laws and regulations.

- Dealing with direct actions by citizens: "ballot box zoning," initiatives and referenda, lawsuits, lobbying, advocacy, expressions of opinion at public hearings or through the media, etc.

- Orchestrating formal citizen participation in policy- and plan-making.

The Service Function of Public Planning Agencies

Jobs in the public sector, especially at the local government level (municipal, county, township, special or regional district), include serving the needs of citizens seeking information, guidelines, permits, or instructions on how to comply with rules and regulations outlined in ordinances or statutes. Normally there is little that is strictly political about the day-to-day exercise of these governmental functions, except when something goes wrong—for example, someone issues a complaint or files a lawsuit in response to an action taken or not taken by the agency.

Nevertheless, you need to be aware of the political minefields that exist in most public settings. If you are a staff planner at a public agency, you're unlikely to be a responsible party to a dispute or action, but you will want to remember that the simplest misjudgment or dispersal of the slightest bit of misinformation about the rules or regulations can turn political if a particularly aggrieved person knows how to make it so. (That same person may also determine if the misinformation has legal as well as political consequences.) And your boss, as the agency's responsible person, surely can be pulled into a situation that may have been of your making (albeit, one would hope, unwittingly).

The simplest misjudgment can turn political if a particularly aggrieved person knows how to make it so.

You need to provide the best possible service and do so in a helpful and full-disclosure manner. Every citizen deserves (and pays for) the service that staff is supposed to provide. You are also obliged to find ways to cope with the inevitable difficult citizen or permit applicant, to treat everyone fairly and equitably, to avoid situations that might turn political unnecessarily, and to keep scrupulous records of what conversations occurred or agreements were made of which you are a part or for which you are in part responsible.

That said, the only things strictly political about the public service-providing function are that (a) something can go wrong and the consequences may be political, and (b) the staffing and funding of this function always occur as a part of the budgeting process, and debating and adopting budgets are inherently political acts.

Direct Citizen Actions

Direct citizen actions can take many forms: formal protests about a planning or public policy action or rezoning proposal, the filing of petitions for or against a proposed action, ballot box zoning, the filing of initiatives and referenda, special-interest lobbying, advocacy of a cause by an interest group, expressions of points of view at public hearings, expressions of opinion through the media, pressure directed at elected officials to do something (or not to do something), recall movements against errant public officials, and lawsuits. Such actions may be initiated by one citizen or a few, sometimes in concert with or on behalf of many others.

Sometimes these actions may seem to be blatantly self-serving and narrow. But there is nothing wrong with such actions in a democratic society, and provisions must be made for citizens to express themselves as best they can. Often such actions are broad-based and legitimate expressions of citizen rights, authority or power—even when they are also forms of political maneuvering or harassment that are not easy for everyone to endure with equanimity. (You will probably have an especially negative reaction if you prefer to maintain an objective stance or stay out of the fray, or find argument and dispute distasteful.)

Sometimes one or two citizens may initiate an action that others will not be willing to champion. On the other hand, the issue they raise may have much merit and may open eyes, stimulate participation, or force a decision-making body to undertake new studies leading to new policies or ways of doing things—and all of that can be good. In California, for example, state statutes give citizens specific standing to bring legal action against local governments for their failure to comply with certain land use and environmental laws or procedures. Citizens and citizen groups are increasingly assertive about taking advantage of these opportunities to force local governments to do what they are supposed to do.

In many states citizens are empowered by their constitutions to initiate legislation to advance a specific cause that, for one reason or another, elected officials have ignored or steered clear of. And citizens may otherwise force actions that they perceive to be essential and unlikely to get off the ground without grassroots action. For example, in Boston (and in other American cities) grassroots citizens' action has caused the mayor and councilors to initiate a successful Main Street program to preserve, bring vitality to, and redevelop a central city neighborhood that would otherwise have languished and been ignored by city hall and the property investment community. Local planners must be able to "go with the flow" when these kinds of forces are energized and then join in the cast of actors.

Some professional planners can become part of the problem if they have not been conducting their agency's business as provided by law, or in an equitable and fair manner, or do not know how to respond to community demands for some kind of action. They should not be surprised if citizens discover the agency's weaknesses, file protests, petitions, or lawsuits to right wrongs as they see them, or initiate corrective actions—using political skills that even they the citizens did not know they had.

Some public-sector or consulting planners may be assigned to work with citizen groups, in which case they must be ready to enter the fray. At a minimum, that means providing assistance as may be required, and even in some cases helping citizen groups achieve their goals if they are consistent with the client's (however "client" may be defined—see Chapter 5 for more on this). In other cases, professional planners will be on the staff of citizen organizations or advocacy groups, or on the staff of private project proponents, or they may work for the consultants who are on contract to such entities.

In the process of exercising their power, citizens may act as individuals with or without professional assistance (e.g., from planning consultants, engineers, attorneys). They may be blessed with advocacy and lobbying skills learned along the way. More often than not, where matters of substantial consequence are at stake, well-exercised citizen power hinges on a few devoted individuals who developed those skills over time and who have made a difference one or more times already. Some are private individuals, others representatives of special-interest organizations on a mission. Their successes have been possible because, in the long run, many people (or just enough people) were grateful for their work and signed on as supporters, and because, so very often, they were dynamos: clever, well-prepared, well-organized, determined, persistent, and equipped to outwit and outlast naysayers, the indifferent, and the opposition.

"To achieve, one must dream greatly, and one must not be afraid to think large thoughts." —
Rachel Carson,
American author and ecologist

The Makings of Citizen Power

When citizens exercise their power creatively and successfully, it is usually because of the following:

- There is a small group of outstanding, well-regarded, and highly committed dynamic leaders who are on a mission and who rarely falter in the face of the inevitable stumbling blocks and the opposition.

- The group can gain access to information that is not already public (e.g., unpublished data, maps, documents, facts, and files), and that details just about everything needed to describe the situation or project in depth.

- There is a clearly articulated vision, and, if appropriate, a plan of action.

- The group knows how to work with others in positive and non-threatening ways, how to recruit supporters, and how to gain the cooperation of key technical, financial, and political people, wherever and whoever they may be.

- Support groups or allies have been or can be lined up as needed and when needed.

- The group leaders have well-honed political skills and political contacts that produce results and support (including public or private funding when needed).

- Communication among the various actors is consistent, regular, unambiguous, and articulate.

- Credit is given generously, often, and publicly to everyone who works on behalf of the cause and provides real help. (Everyone likes being recognized, thanked, and flattered.)

Recent examples of successful citizen actions include ballot initiatives to protect environmental assets; measures to kill a private development project permit that was ill-considered or unpopular; and a new baseball park that proposed use of public funds.

Orchestrating Citizen Participation

Not so long ago, as recently as the early 1970s, it was not universally commonplace to assemble citizens advisory committees during plan-making processes. Public hearings at the end of a plan-making process were often considered adequate opportunities for the public to be heard. These were heady days when abundant monies were available for local planning, much of it from federal agencies, redevelopment and urban renewal funds, and highway building trust funds. The money was easy to come by, and planners, engineers, and redevelopment officials had the funds and the license to plan, clear slums, redevelop, build public housing, and lay down new roads and highways. After all, these experts knew best, and citizens often were regarded as nuisances; they were expected to remain passive and grateful.

Things began to change in the 1970s, with the advent of various grassroots environmental movements, the associated public awareness of planning issues, and the reaction of inner-city residents to heavy-handed urban renewal efforts. Today one would not dare proceed with even rudimentary plan-making without considering citizens as integral participants in the process. As citizens demanded to participate, they also established organizations and learned to lobby and to be political, or they created nonprofit single-purpose organizations that championed causes and sought to accomplish goals on behalf of their members or a common cause. The role of citizens is no longer a passive one, and public hearings today are the last stop in a full array of activities involving citizens in policy-making and in the exercise of political and economic power.

While the process has changed for the better since the early days, and citizen activists demand to participate as never before, some technical experts or elected officials are not overjoyed about or very receptive to what they perceive as interference in the work of the "experts." It may surprise you to find that even today some politicians, as well as many technicians, do not like having to deal with the public, or having the public look over their shoulders, or having to answer phone calls, or being forced to listen to citizen complaints, admonitions, and demands. In fact, in their heart of hearts many would prefer the good old days, when there was little citizen participation, few citizen committees, no public workshops, no citizen lawsuits, no Sierra Club activists, and only perfunctory public hearings. True, planning and decision-making processes can be cumbersome, time-consuming and arduous.

We are obliged to deal with citizen participation and legitimate citizen power, and so are elected officials.

Sometimes one can't help but wonder if selected members of the public will ever tire out and shut up, or just go away. After all, isn't the objective to have the elected officials make decisions and get on with the project or whatever is on the agenda for consideration and action?

On the contrary, we are obliged to deal with citizen participation and legitimate citizen power—and so are the elected officials. There is no short-circuiting the process, and it is only right that this be the case. The land, the environment, our roads and byways, and the social milieus in which we live do belong to the citizens, and they have made it clear since at least the 1970s that they intend to direct the management of their assets. Planners are often looked upon as well as equipped to lead the way in fostering the role of citizens in the policy-making, planning, and plan implementation processes. (See also the section "Who Is the Client?" in Chapter 5.)

Here are some guidelines to follow in situations where you are engaged in any activity involving the orchestration of genuine citizen participation in policy- or plan-making:

Scheduling Meetings. Civic meetings, workshops, and public hearings should be scheduled at times convenient for a majority of the citizens—which usually means evenings and not during the day when the convenience of the staff and some decision-makers might best be served.

Do not schedule or attend meetings that have not been properly noticed and opened to the public as required by law. (Check your jurisdiction's or state's statutes or the bylaws of your organization.) Many states have adopted regulations (known as open meeting laws) prohibiting most decision-making in venues other than in a public place after proper public notice. Many of these laws also prohibit a majority of any elected body from meeting at all in situations that are or have the appearance of being secret and for the purpose of making decisions outside or away from the public (for example, at a local coffee shop or in a member's home).

Providing Information. If your agency asks for citizen participation in the development of a program or plan, or agrees to it upon your recommendation, much effort must go into establishing systems, procedures, avenues of communication, methods for getting input, and ways of getting written material into the hands of the participating citizens in a timely manner. Your agency should deliver reports to members of a citizens advisory committee (CAC), and to the governing body, well before their next meeting so that they have ample time to review documents in advance.

Fact-finding, analytic, progress, and policy or programming reports ought to be full-disclosure documents and prepared and presented so that everyone has all of the same information.

Providing Opportunities to Participate. When establishing the membership of a CAC, make every effort to be inclusive so that all interested parties are represented, listened to, and genuinely able to participate and to contribute their ideas and skills.

If you treat a CAC as a mere rubber stamp of staff predilections and positions, you will nourish resentments. What CAC members want are genuine opportunities to participate from the very beginning and to be paid attention to. In some cases the best results are achieved when the committee, rather than staff, makes formal presentations to the governing body.

Encouraging "Real" Participation. Scheduled public hearings on a proposed course of action are not a substitute for genuine citizen participation throughout a process. Contemporary citizens do not want to be asked to go through the motions of appearing at a meeting and being "allowed" to comment after all of the work has been done by staff or elected officials. They want to be in on the action from the very beginning. They want to arrive at public hearings, most of which are mandated by local or state laws as the last step in the plan-making process, as recognized co-authors and participants in the process of producing the material that is the subject of the public hearing and subsequent action by the governing body.

Beware of tendencies of some public agencies to avoid deferring to the public and the public's rightful desire to give input. Make sure that meeting agendas aren't too tight, and that there is enough time for comments and genuine participation. Public hearings are no place to enforce the commonplace three-minutes-per-speaker rule. It's always better to err in favor of letting everyone have their complete say, and a mistake to quash participation. Bear in mind that there are many citizen participation methods worth considering and that no single method is preferred for all circumstances. The job of the planner is to know which method to employ, and if it does not work to know when and how to change course.

"I do not rule Russia; ten thousand clerks do."
—Nicholas I
(1796-1855)

WORKING WITH POLITICIANS

Some planning jobs involve working directly for or with political figures. For our purposes, "political figures" include non-profit organizational board members, appointed members of public boards and commissions (such as city or county planning commissions, social service or public health boards, park and recreation commissions), elected local politicians (mayors, city council members, county commissioners, or supervisors), elected or appointed members of regional agencies, appointed members of state regulatory commissions (such as public utility commissions, coastal or river preservation commissions), highway and transportation agency members whether appointed or elected, state legislators, and governors.

A politician's decisions may be logical, reasonable, internally consistent and based on the evidence and existing laws—or they may be based on purely political considerations and expedience.

In all cases these people have the right and duty to make near-final or final decisions. These decisions may be logical, reasonable, internally consistent and based on the evidence and existing laws—or they may be based on purely political considerations and expedience. In most cases it will be some intricate combination of all of the above. One never knows in advance what to expect. Never!

Men and women in such positions of ultimate power may be abstractions if you work backstage, but very real forces to contend with if you are in a senior or top professional or management position or are employed as an aide to those who are so positioned. These political figures are your chief clients, or the chosen representatives of the citizens or organizational memberships who are.

If you are a political person's assistant or an adviser, you may report directly to a mayor, board or commission chairperson, or state legislator, separated only by an executive director, city manager, or CEO. Or you may be one or two persons removed. At such a senior or near-senior level, you will be pretty directly affected by the attitudes, beliefs, policy positions, personalities, and behavior of the top people. As a more junior staff member, early in your career, you are likely to become aware of how politics work and how politicians behave, but not be directly involved. Nevertheless, you need to become familiar with how political happenings impinge on the work you are doing either indirectly or directly. Inevitably you will develop your own unique notions and strategies about how to function successfully in political settings—should that be your bent, want, or fate.

For example, you may find that a politician is putting pressure on you to make a certain recommendation, or creating other interference. What should you do? If you are a junior staff member, the logical step is to tell this person that you will discuss the matter with your supervisor. If you are the supervisor, you will have to tell the politician whether what he or she wants is possible or not. Be aware of the differences in your roles: you are in charge of applying the rules, while the politician has the power to enact and change them.

All people in positions of power are, in effect, politicians to one degree or another and at one time or another. They may or may not be governed by principle, or codes of conduct with which you are familiar. On occasion, you may discover that their personal or political agendas have less to do with your agenda (or the agenda of your agency, organization, or firm) than you would expect or hope. One hopes that three out of five on a decision-making body will be receptive, agreeable, reasonable, and in sync with what you want to see accomplished. On the other hand, a month later there might be only two votes. And it's not uncommon for a mayor or CEO or board chairperson to manipulate a meeting agenda, or some of the members of the board, or your department's budget, either to push forward a project of yours or to postpone or kill it. One never can be sure, nor does one always know why.

In another daunting scenario, you may find that at a crucial board or council meeting where an issue is being debated or an important decision is at stake, 20 or so angry citizens show up to vent their feelings and to force a change of thinking in (read: change the votes of) one or more board members. And they may be successful. All of this and more happens.

The list of examples could go on and on. They are not intended to portray the politics of planning in negative or cynical terms, however. They are meant only to illustrate the simple proposition that when your work leaves the realm of analysis, policy-recommending, logic, and reason, you enter an arena where politicians reign and the counting of votes matters. Where special-interest groups go into full gear, anything can happen for any number or reasons. This simply is politics in a democratic society, and often it is very messy indeed. Remember that while there may be times when the results of your work fail to please the politicians, or are off the mark, or require compromises that do not suit you, there are likely to be an equal number of ringing successes.

When your work leaves the realm of analysis, policy-recommending, logic, and reason, you enter an arena where politicians reign and the counting of votes matters.

If all of this terrifies or offends you, it may be wise to reconsider how you want to map out your planning career. And it bears repeating that there are opportunities in the planning field to work successfully and happily well removed from the political fray characterized here. (See examples in Chapter 1, "The Planning Profession and You.") Bear in mind, however, that what may offend or terrify you the first time around and at the beginning of your career may very well come easily as you gain experience. You may even learn that you find the politics of planning to be the most exhilarating and rewarding part of your job.

ADVOCACY AND LOBBYING

The role of advocate in the policy- and plan-making process is a significant one. While most planners may not cast themselves in such terms, being an advocate is precisely what planners must do in order to advance their ideas and proposals, or the proposed projects, policies, and plans of their clients. Public- and private-sector planners rally citizen and decision-maker support for a plan; consultants may do the same and also defend controversial report recommendations; and nonprofit groups lobby politicians and others on behalf of a project or a cause. Some may feel an ethical responsibility to conduct advocacy planning, which can mean speaking for the interests of people who may be absent or not participating for one reason or another.

Doing any of the above effectively involves explaining, persuading, and selling, and may involve lobbying as well. It may include preaching to the choir, trying to convince the skeptical, outwitting the opposition, shoring up support from one's natural allies, or all of these. These activities require some well-honed political skills (bearing in mind, of course, that the degree of advocacy expected from you will vary according to where you work and your position there).

You may find employment with or on behalf of neighborhood or community organizations whose purposes are to advance the best interests of their members through community and political action. These organizations may be single or multi-purpose entities concerned with developing affordable housing, preserving open space or historic resources, programming land trusts, planning redevelopment projects (or stopping them), establishing child care facilities or charter schools, or fostering transportation improvements. Your job may include being chief spokesperson for the group, or advocate, before boards, commissions, and financial institutions. You may help the group organize for political action, or may be expected to help secure outside funding, or prepare action programs and strategies. Your job may include being the group's principal representative before decision-making bodies; if so, it's inevitable that the role you play is going to be at least partially a political one.

If and when you are readying yourself to advance a cause or project, as team member or leader, as a planning director, CEO, or chief administrative officer, or as a consultant, you are putting yourself in a position of advocate and salesperson for what you believe is appropriate (or are paid to believe is appropriate) and for what is supposed to be in your client's best interests. Good ideas and well-crafted proposals do not necessarily stand, endure, or sell themselves on their merits alone. In fact, they rarely do. They need to be explained and defended, and sold in the marketplace. Seasoned professionals learn how to do this through trial and error and, in effect, add lobbying and advocacy to their inventory of skills. Plan-making is comparatively easy; the kind of strategic planning that is implied by advocacy and lobbying is a much bigger challenge.

Below are some guidelines on how to carry out the advocacy/lobbying function. As with most things, doing this successfully means largely accomplishing what you set out to do. There will be occasions, however, when you will try your best and yet run into solid walls of opposition and political maneuvering. It does not follow, though, that you performed poorly or made the wrong tactical choices. It may mean that the decisions or votes went against you due to the politics of the situation or the ideological bents of the decision-makers, or for other reasons, some of which may seem quite unfathomable and some of which may be just the luck of the draw. It's even possible that what you advocate, or the way you present it, is ill-considered and warrants being tabled, rejected, or reconsidered. Don't expect to win them all.

> *Good ideas and well-crafted proposals do not necessarily stand, endure, or sell themselves on their merits alone. They need to be explained and defended, and sold in the marketplace.*

Preparing Yourself

Success in selling ideas and plans, or in representing your client, whether as a public or private advocate, entails:

- Being demonstrably better informed than anyone else on site. This means having the latest and best facts available as well as carefully honed understandings of your point, policy or plan and of the situation and its politics.

- Being confident, poised, and articulate, quick on your feet, skilled at fielding questions, including hostile ones, consummately professional, of good disposition and humor, a good listener, and not defensive.

- Being able to remember and employ the names of the key decision-makers or people with whom you are meeting and to engage them directly and with certitude in connection with the issues at hand.

- Avoiding any semblance of an attitude, such as arrogance, impatience, contempt, or condescension, that may alienate people.

- Perfecting the role of educator, which requires time and patience, an ability to listen, and a strategy for conveying information and messages with clarity and certitude.

Tricks of the Trade

In addition to these fundamental guidelines, it usually pays to learn and implement a few tricks of the trade, the sum of which may make the difference between accomplishing your goals or not.

It is assumed that as advocate you will be quite clear about what you are advocating on behalf of your client. Among the techniques you might consider are the following:

Developing a Strategy. Employ a convincing and winning strategy for progressing systematically toward achievement of your client's goals. You will want to sketch one out and figure out how to implement your strategy. This will include how to present yourself and your findings; whom to lobby and how; what the timing needs to be; and what resources, including human resources, funds, written material, visual displays, expert witnesses, and so on are required to succeed.

Meeting With Decision-Makers. Prepare yourself for face-to-face conversation with each significant decision-maker. This fosters more candid and open discussions than can occur at a public meeting. Such meetings ought to occur at the beginning of a process and, at a minimum, once again just before you wrap up any recommendations. One purpose is for you to listen and learn; another is to test the feasibility of your ideas and proposals before they get solidified, into print, and within the grasp of the media; and still another is to sell your proposal to the decision-makers in a setting that fosters candor and a good discussion.

You want to do this before your material is so solidified that it is perhaps not readily modified. Sometimes the best way to do so is to meet key people for lunch in some neutral place. Doing so is a trust-building exercise that can pay off when the decision-maker is faced with having to make a decision at a public meeting. You want him or her to feel that it is safe to place trust in you as a consequence of having spent time with you and having been able to trust your veracity and judgment so far. By the way, the day you lose this trust, for whatever reason, is the day your project can be in jeopardy and possibly the day you fail to get a vote of confidence and continuing support for the work you have been doing. (More planning directors and CEOs lose their jobs for having lost the trust of their councils or boards than for any other reason.) Moreover, what decision-makers loathe most are surprises, especially those that are unveiled at public meetings. So, these get-togethers and the trust-building they foster must include being sure that decision-makers are well informed in advance of what you are doing, thinking, and proposing. If you are a consultant, this will become standard operating procedure.

If you are an agency staff planner, it will be a tricky business to know your place while implementing your strategic plan successfully. Whether you are a consultant or an agency staff planner, never forget that politicians thrive on being credited publicly and often for their contributions to that which is coming up for consideration (no matter how slight or abundant those contributions may be in your eyes).

Courting the Media. Save for being part of a horrible accident, people are known to fear public speaking the most. (We assume that you will get over this in time, if this is your fear. Or that you will reconsider your place in professional practice.) In the context of policy- and plan-making, number three on the list surely must be saying the "wrong" thing to a newspaper reporter or in a television interview.

It takes years to learn how to court and manipulate the media effectively. At some point you will want to master the art of controlling the information and ideas you have generated and for which you are responsible and likely to be held accountable. Most of this you will learn through practice, but here are a few guidelines:

- Unless you have a well-prepared strategy for disseminating information crucial to nurturing public awareness of and support for your project, don't be carelessly spontaneous, and don't volunteer too much information. What you say may end up in tomorrow's newspaper and in a form not to your exacting standards. Beware of what you say.

- If you truly want media attention, however, be sure to prepare news releases in writing. Well-thought-out "quotables" may be exactly what you want the media to hear and print. These people crave one-liners and points that lend themselves to being printed or broadcast as direct quotes from you.

- Similarly, if you are expecting a call from a reporter or a visit from a television crew, plan out what you are going to say ahead of time. Try to think in short sentences that are easy to remember and quote. Try to anticipate questions and have responses ready.

- If you don't have the information requested, say you will provide it by a specific time and then do so.

TO SUM UP: HONING YOUR POLITICAL SKILLS

Faced with expressions of citizen power, or the machinations of politicians and other decision-makers, you and anyone else in a professional position will muster all sorts of often-conflicting responses—understanding, cooperation, empathy, patience, revulsion, enthusiasm, tongue-biting—depending on how well specific exercises of political power correspond with your own attitudes and with the existing policies, rules, and regulations that are supposed to govern planning decisions. How you deal with citizens and politicians will depend in part on your own tastes and values, and on your commitments to rational argumentation and decision-making processes.

You can be sure that in the context of a citizen's frustration over some glitch in the pursuit of funds, a permit, a license, or some sort of entitlement, there is going to be tension, raw emotion, perhaps even heavy-duty politics, and sometimes very limited room for predictability. In the context of creative planning there will be surprises, delays, expressions of delight and support mixed with determined argumentation.

In all cases you must learn to adapt to the situation at hand and to invent coping strategies on the spot. If you are a staff planner for a public agency, remember that you are the representative of the entire governmental body when you are at work with the public. Whether you are neutral or an active actor in these dramas depends on circumstances, your predilections, prevailing ethical standards, your disposition, the specifications of the job, what your boss will tolerate, and how you measure the politics of the situation.

You must learn to adapt to the situation at hand and to invent coping strategies on the spot.

While many of the tasks you will perform may be formally defined as strictly technical or recommending, and seemingly far removed from what decision-makers and political figures do, most planning activities (plan-making, policy-recommending, implementation, enforcement of regulations, design) in reality are inherently political. And political figures (elected or appointed) often make decisions about your work, or about your organization's work, for strictly political reasons—and maybe not on the basis of principle or for high and noble purposes. For better or for worse, majority votes are what count, and the reasons underlying each politician's votes may or may not square with what you perceive to be principled, reasonable, or proper. At other times the exercise of political power may precisely suit you and seem very proper and noble indeed. Let's hope that you bat better than .300 most of the time.

To a greater or lesser degree, depending on the setting in which you work, issues of authority and power are bound to come up. In any community setting, one cannot assume that planning will be free of politics and political action, or of political personalities and behavior, political chicanery, or struggles for political power. On the contrary.

What You Need to Know

So, what do you do and how do you behave when your work is carried on in a politicized setting and may be subject to political machinations? The simple answer is that you adapt. You also recognize the following:

- Your job is first and foremost technical and advisory. You present the facts, lay out alternative courses of action, and prepare policies, plans, and programs. Or, if you are processing development applications, you provide information and the relevant regulations in a straightforward manner. You do so professionally and without any second-guessing about how what you are doing will play politically—save being sure that you are not a party to some huge and unavoidable political flap due to omissions or errors of your making, or due to surprises.

- If you are in a policy-recommending or plan-making role, you will also need to assess the political scene and identify, as best you can, the interest groups, advocates, and opposition groups and the decision-makers most likely to press for one policy or action over another, and who is likely to benefit from one course of action over another. You will also need to determine who is likely to vote one way or another based on ideology, already expressed attitudes and opinions, past history or voting patterns, political party affiliation, or whatever.

What You May Choose to Do

Your best response is to figure out if you have a legitimate and defensible role to play in affecting the outcome of a dispute or issue, and then decide how to go about playing that role, if at all. You may choose to influence the political debate, if there is one, or to become a political force yourself. On the other hand, you may opt to remain benign and keep out of it. Your own sense of values and ethics—and in some cases the extent to which you value your job—may be your only guides in making these choices.

Normally, an overt political role for a public planner is not considered kosher and may even be prohibited. But don't be fooled by what may be regarded as the norm. Many planning officials are inevitably caught up in politics and political battles by virtue of their central role in shepherding projects through the review and approval process. Or they may become political players because they manage a large and powerful agency (or department thereof) with enormous and often discretionary influence or power over huge pieces of public and private real estate and large development or redevelopment projects, or substantial budgets and spending power.

There is likely to be no escape from being caught up in a politicized situation from time to time—and being cast as one of the actors—so it is wise to be prepared. If you are a private consultant representing a client vis-a-vis a governmental agency, you can be sure that you will come face-to-face with political realities of some kind and will need to have sharpened your political skills along the way. (If you are not prepared to do this, it is not advised that you become an independent contractor responsible for plan-making activities within a community setting.) If you are on the staff of a mayor or other political figure, you can be sure that politics will dominate your working environment and how you look at things and function. This is where your own potentially effective and perhaps subtly employed advocacy and lobbying skills will come into play.

A FINAL NOTE

Politics, in the most popular and negative senses, is often regarded as a messy and dirty activity peopled by sometimes marginally likeable and self-absorbed politicians playing political games for their own ends. Consider, though, that politics might also be:

- A legitimate clash of naked power, political-party agendas, and socioeconomic and environmental special-interest forces.

- A real conflict between right and wrong.

- What one pays for, endures, and even hopes for in a democratic society.

- Pure entertainment.

9

Twelve Traps to Avoid

The nice thing about working in a job for awhile is that you get good at it. But there can also be a disadvantage: You start to develop some bad habits. This chapter distills the lessons of the preceding ones by reviewing 12 common traps that people in planning-related fields often fall into—traps that you should avoid.

Trap 1: Dismissing Things as "Just Politics"

Politics are an integral part of most planning work and help to define the culture of a community. The politician's job is different from yours. In making their decisions, politicians usually weigh many different factors, some of which may be at odds with planning concerns. You will probably be most effective in your job if you can develop some appreciation and respect for the role of politics and politicians in the community where you work. At a minimum, try to tolerate the political process—otherwise, you are likely to be unhappy a lot of the time.

An important note: Tolerating and even appreciating politics does not mean giving up completely on the issues you care about and succumbing to political pressures. If your job is to provide professional recommendations and advice, do it. Just try to accept that things won't always go your way, and sometimes politics will be involved. And that sometimes you may be brought into a political drama unwittingly. This is a tricky—but important—mental balancing act. The intricate matter of politics is explored in detail in Chapter 8, "Essential Political Skills."

Trap 2: Being Arrogant or Smug

This may be a corollary of Trap 1. Don't fall into the trap of assuming that you are right all of the time and have all of the answers. And don't tout your academic degrees and achievements publicly, unless you're asked. It's possible that only a small proportion of the people in your audience are as highly educated as you are, and they will not want to be reminded of it by an uppity (and perhaps young) staff person. (In the average community, college graduates make up far less than 50 percent of the adult population.)

You may have valuable training and experience, but other people—even politicians, citizens, and those with no formal planning education—might, too. Keep listening; someone may suggest something you hadn't thought of, or become an ally when you most need one.

That's not to say you shouldn't present your findings and recommendations forcefully and convincingly, or that you shouldn't defend your position. Just try not to display arrogance or impatience, and do not threaten or argue with members of the public. No matter how much you know (or think you know), or how convinced you are of your position, there are almost always alternative points of view, or perhaps even alternative facts, and always alternative ways of doing things. In the long run, the decision makers' job is to weigh the facts and alternatives and draw conclusions as they see fit. Keep trying to influence the decision makers and the outcomes, and you may very well be appreciated for trying. But part of your job will be learning to live with the choices others make.

Trap 3: Assuming That You Know Everything (Or That One Size Fits All)

One of the main criticisms that can legitimately be laid at the feet of many young and not-so-young planners, and other helping and design professionals, is the tendency to carry around a kit bag of favorite notions, ideologies, formulae, and ready-made solutions, and to assume that they can be applied in all or most situations where help is needed or plans required. This is a huge mistake.

Almost everything of any magnitude and significance that you will do is bound to be much more complex than you or anyone else imagined. Count on it. Unknown facts will be uncovered, even though you thought you had assembled them all. Points of view you've never heard of or could even imagine will flow out of the mouths of passionate people in staff meetings and at public hearings. The time estimated to complete a task will be way off, or worse yet much more than the budget allowed. Ways of doing things or solutions that seem sensible and logical to you will prove neither sensible nor logical to others, and the others may have the political power while you have none at all.

One of the biggest mistakes of all is to go into a neighborhood (or national forest, or wetlands area, or Indian reservation) loudly proclaiming that conditions, to your way of thinking, cry out for improvement or some sort of treatment, only to find that the locals do not agree. They may see your perception of the problems (and the solutions) as shallow, incomplete, poorly thought through, off-target, too middle-class (or not middle-class enough), too radical (or not radical enough), economically infeasible, culturally offensive or insensitive, or just dead wrong. And your ideas may be one or all of these, because you applied your own perceptions, values, and preconceptions, or a favorite of someone else's, or a textbook answer, instead of coming up with genuinely appropriate approaches that grew organically from local conditions and were based on what local people wanted and would endorse.

To do the right thing, you must stop, look, and listen. Take your time. Record what you see—and never assume you have seen everything or that others see the same things you do. Talk with and listen to the principals or inhabitants. And then come back in a week, or a month, and do the same thing all over again. Hang out and listen to the locals—in their coffee shops or bowling alleys. Talk one-on-one with fellow professionals on the team and, if appropriate and acceptable to your boss, to appointed and elected officials. Never surprise the latter with a ready-made set of ideas and recommendations. What you propose must be well-thought-out and defensible, and everything must be tested and discussed with all major actors in the policy-making or plan-making drama. Remember, too, that many decision-makers, and especially elected officials, behave differently in a public setting than in any face-to-face, one-on-one meeting, so don't count your chickens before they hatch. Be absolutely sure that you are genuinely hearing what they say to you and what they say in public, and act accordingly.

Trap 4: Believing Too Much in Experts

On the other hand, don't let yourself be overwhelmed by people with multiple degrees and imperious attitudes who are sent in to intimidate you (or who just can't help themselves). Engineers, scientists (biologists, archaeologists, et. al.), attorneys, and academics have a great deal to offer: know-how, expertise, focused perspectives. But as specialists, more often than not, they might have been shortchanged when it comes to a comprehensive view, a planning approach, political acumen, and the skills required to work well and easily with other professionals and with citizens.

People who don't like what you are saying or doing, or how things are progressing, might rally an army of "experts" in an attempt to get their way. Planners can be especially vulnerable to this type of intimidation. Our education and the nature of our work often leave us feeling that we know a little about a lot of things, but not much about anything in particular. And sometimes it's true that others perceive us as "experts in nothing" and therefore vulnerable. Just remember, though, that the generalist, holistic nature of your training has a value of its own: It has given you certain unique skills, which might include being the glue that holds the project together, knowing how to draw the best out of the experts, and being able to distinguish between a valid point and mere bluster. In the words of an anonymous sage, "Perspective is worth 100 IQ points."

Experts who are on your side aren't always right, either. If a specialist on your team is telling you something that just doesn't sound right, don't be afraid to question it. Part of your job is to interpret what the experts say so that ordinary people can understand it. How can you do that if you don't understand it yourself?

Moreover, it is a troublesome reality that members of the public often trust the experts who have recognizable credentials or licenses. Citizens often perceive engineers, geologists, attorneys, and other specialists as having a hold on the truth. It is your job as planner to assert your role and advance your ideas effectively and forcefully in the face of the experts, who are not always right, and their supporters. Keep in mind, too, that often there is more than one expert per issue, and that much of what passes for expert thought, at least on planning-related subjects, is mere opinion or is used to flummox the innocent.

Trap 5: Fearing the Public

Attend enough acrimonious public meetings, and anyone is likely to become a little shell-shocked. (Interestingly, single-purpose experts are often extremely competent up to the moment when they are obliged to deal with citizen groups, even benign ones.)

You will need to determine your own personal tolerance for difficult dealings with the public, and design your work life accordingly. But try not to be afraid of the public. True, the planning process has a way of making private citizens angry, intolerant, and even rude. But these people are still human beings, like you are, and may be far more intimidated by the process (or even by you) than they let on, especially if proposed policies, rules, and regulations threaten their expectations. Often even the slightest sign that you are willing to listen and understand will diffuse a difficult situation.

Among the public (as well as among the experts, politicians, and other planners) will be proponents of ideologies right and left. You cannot expect to change or win over these ideologues, especially if they also have difficult personalities. You can, however, learn to deal with them, neutralize their ideologies if they seem to be less than helpful, or co-opt them into working with you.

Trap 6: Developing Sloppy Writing and Speaking Habits

As you continue in your career, it can be a challenge to keep your writing and speaking clear and jargon-free. Out of convenience or even laziness, you may fall into using certain planning buzzwords. It can also be tempting to employ jargon as a kind of armor to defend yourself against experts and the public (see Traps 4 and 5), thinking that if you use enough technical terms, people may think you really know what you're talking about. That approach often backfires, though. Most people appreciate clear language, and can tell when someone is putting on airs. It takes constant vigilance to maintain clarity in your writing and speaking, but people will notice and reward you for it.

So work hard to develop and maintain your communication skills. Learn (and remember) the difference between "its" and "it's." Try not to use the words "parameter" or "paradigm" (or a host of other jargon-laden words and phrases), especially at a public meeting. Think about who your audience is, and tailor your writing and speaking to communicate with them effectively. Avoid an attitude that fails to be respectful or at least tolerant. And don't take twice the time you need to say something at a meeting or presentation; this almost always betrays to your audience that you are a gasbag or came to the meeting unprepared. Keep it short and sweet. People who need to know more can ask questions.

Trap 7: Trying to Make Your Work "Perfect"

Of course, you want to do the best job possible. You want to re-search thoroughly, understand all the angles, make sure every-thing is buttoned up tight. But planners can become so involved in the details that they lose sight of the big picture. Often, the po-litical process will push things along at a pace that does not cor-respond with your expectations, whether you like it or not (see Trap 1). You will be better off if you learn how to flow with the process. That means knowing when to delay the release of a re-port because something important needs to be worked out, and knowing when to let go. You will develop a sense for this through practice, and by watching your more seasoned col-leagues. (Be aware, though, that there can be a fine line between knowing when to let go and just plain being sloppy. When you're sending something out that's less than perfect, make sure it's be-cause you have to keep the process moving, and not because you're just feeling lazy.)

Trap 8: Missing Deadlines

Perhaps due to the temptations of Trap 7, planners can be no-torious for missing deadlines. This is typically (although not always) more prevalent within a public agency setting than at a consulting firm or other private business. Planning research can often become a kind of bottomless pit; before you know it, your deadline is approaching and you don't have much to show for your efforts.

Time management will probably be one of the less glamorous as-pects of your job, but it's well worth learning (see Chapter 7, "Es-sential Management Skills"). In fact, your first responsibility on a new job is to figure out precisely what you are doing and within what financial and time constraints you are obliged to produce what. While we all learn that the planning process is the essence of planning and plan-making, it is equally important to identify the ultimate products and to know how to get them out on time. Whether you are working in the public, private, or nonprofit sec-tor, the mantra is simple: Time is money.

If you're assigned a project and think you will need help, say so. (Ideally, you will recognize this at the outset, but it's okay to send out an SOS midway through.) If you find yourself becoming mired in a research problem, consult your supervisor or another colleague; just talking about the problem can often illuminate the solution, or at the very least help you chart a graceful way out. Deadlines can be a nuisance, but they are unavoidable and need to be taken seriously. Your work is part of a process—something to keep in mind at all times.

Trap 9: When in Doubt, Convening a Meeting

Some meetings are necessary; others are time-wasters. Try not to become a meeting addict who calls and attends so many gatherings that no actual work gets done. While some managers spend most of their time in meetings, the best ones know how to be judicious with their own, and other people's, precious time. Chapter 7 ("Essential Management Skills") suggests guidelines for deciding when meetings are needed and for making them efficient, useful, and creative events, rather than just time-consuming diversions.

Trap 10: Being Unprepared

Whether you are the sole individual working on a project, or a team member, the time will come for making a progress report to your boss or client. Sooner or later you will stand up at a commission or board meeting, or appear before a city council, or maybe even a state legislative committee or bank loan committee. All eyes will be upon you. You've probably been touted as an expert, or *the* expert. The only reason you are there is to make a presentation or to give testimony, or to defend a report or a policy proposal that you are supposed to know more about than anyone else on the face of the globe. You'd better be ready! And articulate, confident, sharp, well-informed, and non-combative.

Being prepared usually means that you are, and can demonstrate that you are, the most informed person in the room about the topic or agenda item before a board, commission, committee, or council. You know the facts well, you can state the arguments for and against with unimpeachable clarity and certitude, and you have anticipated all contrary arguments and all conceivable questions from both allies and nay-sayers (or virtually all of them, since there are often surprises in settings like this).

Being prepared also means you've done your homework and you've done it thoroughly. It's not just on paper in the form of a formal report or written policy document; it's been absorbed into your brain and being, and you do not need to take a lot of time consulting the document and searching for responses at a meeting. And, more likely than not, you cannot assume that your audience has read your report, or, if they have, that they have interpreted your words as you intended. Being prepared means that you can handle this kind of situation and other surprises that may arise in the midst of your presentation or testimony.

When you start out in your first job, the thought of facing a roomful of people might actually cause you to panic and over-prepare. As you move along through your career, you are likely to find yourself relaxing a bit or even a good deal. Just don't relax too much, and do not assume that you know it all (Traps 2 and 3) or that you do not need to prepare. This attitude could lead to embarrassment and perhaps some form of approbation from your boss or client.

Trap 11: Trying to Survive On Good Intentions Alone

Succeeding in any milieu means not only knowing that you must listen and learn, do your homework, and be prepared. It means crafting a personal way to do these things that leads to satisfactory results. If you carefully examine the achievements of a successful MVP quarterback (the team player), or a five-time Wimbledon champion, or your family ophthalmologist (individuals at work), you will conclude that they would not have made it without self-imposed discipline, endless practice, much experience, diligent focus, and determination. They did much more than merely show up for work each day.

Planning tends to attract people who want to do good for the community or society, or to assist their client in achieving his or her goals, or to do excellent research or design. That means that most people in the planning profession have good intentions; they endorse and want to see results and usually some sort of significant change and betterment. Wanting is good, and good intentions are fine, but wishful thinking and rhetoric are not enough. Translating intentions, goals, and designs—yours and your client's—into measurable results requires the same kind of discipline, focus, and determination that quarterbacks, pro tennis players, and eye surgeons learn on the way to their stellar achievements. Don't just sit back feeling smug—work continually to improve your skills and add new ones.

Trap 12: Getting Discouraged

Just in case the message has not gotten through, good planning work is an art as well as the crafty application of a set of skills. Young planners are burdened with a need to do good, and they believe that the planning world is just the place to do so. Part of the art of planning is to avoid Traps 1 through 11, and another is to keep on trying in the face of the many challenges and obstacles the world has put before you. Planning is tough. And yet it is rewarding and (one would hope) fun if you find the right venue. It's also one of those callings in which you might very well realize only five percent of what you're aiming for—and then again maybe 95 percent. You may not be able to control all the outcomes. In face of the defeats, the slow pace of change, or disappointments, try to maintain a positive attitude by recognizing the limitations inherent in practicing this type of work, and by concentrating on developing and applying your best skills well.

CHAPTER

10

Setting a Career Path for Yourself

After you have been working for a while, whether for a public agency, private firm, or nonprofit organization, you will probably have one or more of the following things on your mind:

- *Does the job still satisfy me?* Salary, vacation, working hours, benefits, compatibility with co-workers, opportunity to work independently and make decisions, office amenities, and the character and intrinsic value of the work to be performed—all must be considered in answering the question.

- *Will the job lead to something better?* Most of us want to be promoted, take on more responsibility, make more money, or gain recognition from our peers and society—or all of the above. Each job up the ladder of success should fulfill our need to progress toward our own personal and professional goals.

- *Am I ready for a new job?* There is bound to be some uncertainty when contemplating a promotion or job change. Do I have the proper education and background? Do I have the required skills? What do the people who are making the hiring or promoting decisions expect me to know and be able to do? Is there a good match between their expectations and my capabilities? Can I learn readily on the job or by taking a night course? Will the demands of a promotion or new job overwhelm me and exceed my capabilities?

- *What sort of venue do I want?* Do I want to stay in the same agency or firm? Or try something and somewhere new? Am I prepared to move myself and my family to another city or state?

All of these are legitimate questions. They are the questions you will ask each time you contemplate or prepare for a change, and they are the questions senior people ask as they consider a position as an agency head or CEO. Everyone is bound to be puzzled by such concerns after having been on the job a while. For many, contemplating or undertaking a career move is a stressful experience, mostly because of uncertainties suggested by these questions. The answers lie within you, and from the outset it may help to have at least a generalized career plan as a guide into the unknown future. This chapter suggests some ways of mapping out that plan, first by suggesting that it is important to decide whether it's time to make a change, and then by suggesting ways for you to figure out what that change should be.

IS IT TIME TO MOVE ON?

"There are some days when I think I'm going to die from an overdose of satisfaction."
—Salvador Dali (1904-1989), Spanish artist

If, as either a relatively short-term employee or someone considerably more senior, you find yourself uneasy about your situation, or have not been experiencing an "overdose of satisfaction," or have been thinking about quitting your current job, it is probably for one or more of the following reasons:

- You've been passed over for a promotion and you're feeling humiliated, demoralized, or both; or there is simply no room higher up in the firm or agency. It's time to get out of the box in which you find yourself.

- The work you are doing is dull or unfulfilling, there are no prospects for better work, and you feel a need to seek out a new opportunity.

- You've identified a new job or type of work that may make sense for you because it offers an opportunity to learn more, do more, and/or earn more.

- You want to retire, perhaps quite early or perhaps after a long and distinguished career, or you want to drop out, travel, go back to school, take some long hard looks at yourself, write poetry, whatever.

- You sense a budget crunch (or other trouble), and you want to quit before being laid off.

- An ethical or moral issue arises and the only honorable way out is to quit. Perhaps whistle-blowing is not appropriate, or nothing can be done to restore truth, honesty, or integrity where it is wanting. Raising a fuss isn't likely to do any good, either. Your options appear to be either to get out gracefully or to write a letter of resignation blasting those you hold responsible for your dilemma or what you see wrong. (Often such actions are quite cathartic but make no significant impact on the agency or firm, or the behavior of those you hold responsible. That said, administrators have been known to quit when they concluded that the board or council was acting irresponsibly or dishonestly, or not paying attention. In any case, quitting on a matter of principle cannot be taken lightly, but it may be precisely the right thing to do under certain circumstances.)

- You've always wanted to be a community development director (or a city manager, or the head of a nonprofit), and it's time to take the logical next step toward achieving that goal.

Getting Mad and Getting Even

From time to time, situations will arise that inspire ire, frustration, self-doubts, or daunting challenges to your professional and ethical standards. People in planning are just as vulnerable as anyone else in that they can be ignored or walked over, passed by, harassed, and publicly humiliated. Sometimes expressing your feelings is exactly the right thing to do. On other occasions, the only answer may be to file a formal complaint or to quit. Getting mad at the client or boss, or a member of the public, or the mayor, is risky business. There are no guidelines for most situations, and you will have to muddle through as best you can, being true to yourself, of course.

Seasoned planners agree that there are times—jolly good times—when you can fashion a strategy that outwits those who mistreat you. If that seems possible, then, by all means do so. Sometimes, outwitting the opposition will give you the greater satisfaction. On other occasions, it might be necessary to engage in some subtle political maneuvering of your own.

There may be times, too, when you aren't thinking about quitting (yet), but are aware of feeling stressed, frustrated, or unhappy. This might be for any one or more of the following reasons:

- You are no longer having fun with the work you are doing. (Disillusionment is a common affliction among planners and others in idealistic professions.)

- You have too much work to do, or too much pressure.

- Your employer is not giving you recognition for your accomplishments, especially in meaningful terms such as pay raises.

- You are in a job that is beyond your capabilities and you are in denial about it, or you know it and can't figure out what to do about it.

- Your boss has different things in mind for you (in terms of assignments, working hours, compensation, level of responsibility or authority, future prospects, etc.) than you do for yourself.

- Your boss is a jerk and you don't want to wait around for the better times that will arrive after his or her retirement day 15 years from now.

- Your co-workers are jerks and make dreadful nine-to-five companions.

- You know you are unfulfilled and that other and better jobs (or even careers) are out there for which you are qualified—but it's easier to stay where you are, or the options are limited, or you are invested in a can't-be-beat retirement plan, or you'd have to sell your house and move the kids to new schools— and it eats away at you and probably affects the quality of your work.

- After testing the waters in a variety of positions and settings over a period of years, you now know precisely what niche would suit your personality and professional needs—and your present job is not the right niche for you.

- You sense that you have not yet found your niche, and you don't know what to do about it.

First, some advice, given any of the above circumstances: Don't quit too soon. Consider keeping your present job while you look for another. This strategy continues your income and your security. It also demonstrates to a prospective new employer that you are making a job change voluntarily—and not petulantly.

That said, quitting and changing jobs (unless done too often within a short period of time, or for strictly petulant reasons) is nothing to feel awkward about. Quitting can and should be a creative act under most circumstances. A job move may be just a link, and a legitimate one, in a chain of career changes. While the holding power of a benefits package, pension, and seniority rights can be enormous, professional and executive job changes and dropouts are commonplace. It's worth noting, too, that the trend is moving away from traditional, long-term employment; holding a job for a shorter time, or holding more than one job at once, has become far more common than it was a generation ago. That's not to say you're obligated to follow the trend—just that you need not feel bad about experiencing the need to move on.

TAKING STOCK

If you want to redirect or restart your career, it's time to make a career plan. This begins with noting your current skills. You are likely to be impressed, and others might be, too. These skills are undoubtedly marketable if you know how to sell them and yourself, match them with available job opportunities, and show a prospective employer how your education, experience, and skills can help him or her out. Remember: You must have something to offer—and it's very likely that after some years on a job and after some seasoning you are an impressive commodity for a new employer's consideration. You must also genuinely believe you have something to offer, and you must know how to sell yourself and your package of attributes in the competitive marketplace.

What are your skills, and how might a new employer use them?

Taking stock of yourself, and then planning your next move, may send you back to the first few chapters of this book. Where do you see yourself fitting in the planning profession? What are your skills, and how might a new employer use them? How can you secure the job you want? To those questions, you might add a new one that may have emerged after a few years (or more) on

154   *A Career Worth Planning*

the job: Are you ready to change careers and get out of planning altogether? For some, this is a realistic question. For others, it never comes into play.

No one formula for career planning works for everyone. Bear in mind that your particular needs are individual and specific and will depend on what you already know, what new skills you want to learn and perfect, your personality and aptitudes, and where you see yourself going.

First, you need to accept the notion that there is not room for everyone at the top, nor does everyone want to be there. Not only are a lot of people employed in middle management, but they are needed there—and many are very content there. If you do not aspire to be the chief executive officer (CEO) or his or her deputy, you should not allow yourself to be targeted into the kinds of situations where becoming a supervisor and then the boss is inevitable. Decide what is right for you and then place the job of career planning and development in your own hands.

Decide what is right for you and then place the job of career planning and development in your own hands.

After a few years on the job, it will probably become apparent to you what your work preferences really are, what you like and dislike doing, what your strengths are, what you need to learn to do better, what the keys to advancement are, and what you can and should do next. When you know the answers to these questions, you are ready to determine whether to stay where you are or move on. Here are the characteristics about yourself that you will want to take stock of.

Your Skills

The first thing to do is look at yourself and find answers to this question: what are my skills and what do I most prefer doing, or what would I most prefer doing in the future once I pass through the journeyman/woman stage and have honed my skills a bit? Choose from among those we have discussed in this book: generalist; specialist; social-personal (people); communication; work programming, budgeting and time management; stylistic; research; new technology; management; political; lobbying; and working with citizens and exercising or helping others exercise citizen power (see Chapter 2, "What Employers Are Looking For"). Obviously these are not mutually exclusive categories, and everyone has his or her own mix of skills, aptitudes, tastes, and druthers.

Your Likes and Dislikes

Here we are referring to the things you like to do—or now think
you might like to do—versus the things you avoid for whatever
reasons, and the things that just don't describe who you are and
what you will want to do in the future. You may have skills or potential in some areas and yet simply do not want to exercise
them. You need to know what they are so you do not make the
mistake of taking on responsibilities that cause you to confront
demons that will impair your work, advancement, and well
being. Bear in mind that some people like to do research and
work quietly at their desks, while others may be qualified to do
research but are unfulfilled if they are not out among people attempting to sell a project to the public or to decision-makers. Do
you know for sure what your likes and dislikes are? It might be
a good idea to list them.

Your Strengths

Putting aside for a moment your likes and dislikes as you now
know them, since tastes change over time, what are your inner
strengths? What do you know for sure are your real strengths as
a person and as a professional? Do you have a gift for gab? Do
words flow easily out of your word processor? Are you at home
out in the wilderness and capable of almost intuiting what nature
is doing? Are you a facilitator who can get things done and get
other people to do things that need to be done?

Whether or not you know the answers now, it will be time one
day to face up to them—and that will be all to the good as you
prepare for your future. This is the part of any self-evaluation exercise that requires you to be honest with yourself and under no
illusions. There are no right answers to these questions. It's all a
matter of knowing who you are and then going on from there. It
is highly likely that whoever you are there is a place for you to do
the work that you are skilled at and destined for—and will enjoy.

Your Work Style

All of these skills, strengths, likes, and dislikes usually translate
into a personal working style and a working environment that
you prefer. Are you someone who likes the security of staying
with one employer for a long time, possibly until retirement? Do
you have unlimited ambition, and thrive on big challenges and
risk-taking? (These are people who become planning directors or

city managers, then move on to executive directorships of state agencies, and then move on to the next big challenge.) Are you the restless type, who likes to move from the public to the private sector, do a little of this and a little of that, consult and then teach, or do both at once, and so on? Do you prefer producing things, or managing or orchestrating other people? Do you savor and thrive on control, or are you just as happy not being the boss? Do you prefer working inside, outside, on the streets of the community, in the office or at home, all day or all night, on a team or alone? Are you satisfied with the intellectual scope of the planning field, or do you see planning as a stepping stone to other things (social work, law, running for political office, etc.)?

What You Still Need to Know

Do you know what skills you want to improve on to accomplish your goals, to advance, or to survive? For example, there may be research methods that are required of you and that interest you but that are not in your present repertory. Or perhaps your speaking skills are less than adequate. There are many opportunities at local colleges for post-graduate adult education, and that is where you may want to begin. It may be a matter of self-study or emulating a mentor. The real benefits, however, seem to come less from classrooms and classroom drill than from the exposure to new ideas and the chance to compare notes with peers. This exposure can come to you at conferences and in other settings where you are in contact with fellow professionals. Do not overlook what is to be gained by spending time with people in allied professions who come to any project or assignment with perspectives that differ from yours and who have knowledge and skills that can rub off on you (and vice versa). By all means, much of what you need to learn is going to emerge within the working environment through trial and error. You will learn from listening to and observing others, and having your ideas tested in meetings with fellow professionals. You will also learn at public meetings, where anyone who is unprepared will be discovered, where the learning curve is likely to be rapid and of genuine value to you and your growth, and where being accomplished at what you do will, as a rule, be noticed.

STAKING OUT YOUR CAREER PATH

Making a career plan goes hand in hand with the process of taking stock and improving yourself. In this section we do not suggest a model for everyone to adopt and follow, since that is up to you. The process of making and implementing your career plan has to be highly individualized. But, we do suggest things that you can do to help yourself as you settle into your career and ponder moving onward and upward.

First, try to define what you like and don't like about your current job. This is especially important if you feel stuck in a box on the organizational chart with no place to go, or find you don't want to advance to the next logical place. Set down in writing those aspects of the job, and the functions you perform, that you like and perform well. What skills and working conditions should prevail to make your work more fun and satisfying, more useful, and more productive? Will it be possible to fulfill those desires in your current workplace? If you were to acquire new skills to do your current job better, what would they be? What would you gain by having these new skills? Do you want to have them? What types of jobs would they logically lead to?

This exercise should help you decide whether you ought to stay with your current employer. If the answer appears to be "no" (or even "maybe"), your next step is to explore jobs and career directions you're really interested in. You may not know exactly what those are yet; in fact, you may only have the smallest inkling of how your skills might correspond with a new job or speciality. What's important is to get out and about, through any or all of the means listed below. By all means, do not make yourself scarce or forgotten, and be prepared for serendipitous happenings leading to magical opportunities.

Going to Conferences

Conferences can be invaluable information and networking venues for people who are rethinking their careers. If you still don't know where you want to work next, conferences give you a chance to hear what others are doing, and think about how your skills might match up with a new job or specialty. If you already have some ideas for your next step, you can make useful contacts. Regardless of your current circumstances, you will probably meet at least some people who work outside your usual network of contacts, and who will be more willing to talk about their work than they would be back at the office. (Note: Consider going to conferences other than those aimed strictly at people in your own field, just to see what else is going on and what opportunities might present themselves.)

Informational Interviews

Many people will be flattered that you are interested in the work they do. Set up appointments with them to learn about their jobs and what they did to get themselves to the place where they are now. Important note: It's usually best to treat these as information-gathering, not job-seeking, sessions. Of course, you may be pleasantly surprised if one of your contacts offers you a job on the spot. Your college or university department may be able to put you in contact with alumni whose jobs interest you.

Seeking Out a Mentor

There may be one person, or a handful of people, who represents a career ideal for you, or who is especially helpful in providing you with direction. See if these people are willing to have you check in with them from time to time for guidance, support, brainstorming, etc.

Seeking Out a Headhunter

If you have a clear idea of the type of work you want to do, a headhunter might be able to lead you directly to it, or have new possibilities that never would have occurred to you. Some head-hunters specialize in public-sector recruiting, and others private sector. University career planning offices, career counseling services, and your other contacts can probably help you locate a headhunter (or maybe one has already located *you*).

Volunteering

If you identify a place where you think you might like to work, see if you can get a volunteer (or even part-time paid) position there. This will give you a chance to get to know the organization and the work they do, and decide if it's for you.

Continuing Your Education

Taking a class in a subject you're interested in allows you to find out more about it without giving up your present job and diving into something new that might not be right for you after all.

Self-Education

Learn as much as you can about yourself and the career directions and jobs that interest you. This may mean reading lots of current affairs newsmagazines, subscribing to community or special-interest newsletters, reading books that can give you insight into the society you are seeking to join, or visiting with people at the coffee shop in the community where you want to work. Or it may mean spending several weekends immersed in a pile of self-help books. The idea is to avoid feeling inactive, stuck, isolated, closed-minded, remote, at arm's length, indifferent, or too comfortable and safe at your present desk.

Seeking Career Counseling

Many career counseling services offer diagnostic tests, resume critiques, job-finding services, networking opportunities, and so on. A possible downside of this approach: most career counselors are not especially familiar with the planning profession, and therefore may not fully understand the skills you offer and the type of work you are seeking. Nonetheless, you may find some value in the more general services these places provide—especially if you are thinking about dropping out of planning and moving on to something totally new.

Sabbaticals/Travel

Your current employer might be willing to grant you a sabbatical, during which you work somewhere else and return with knowledge useful to your organization. This might give you a fresh perspective, or an opportunity to learn about a job that interests you without quitting your current one. For example, try contacting the American Planning Association (APA) for information about continuing education and international job exchange programs. Some planners have visited counterparts on the job in other countries for a few weeks (or longer), and then hosted those people back at home for the same length of time. This might be a chance to travel, gain some perspective on your job, learn about how planning works in another country, remain open to new ideas and ways of doing things, and make some new friends. Some universities and other institutions also offer continuing education abroad and fellowship programs that may allow you to broaden your horizons.

Alternatively, if your personal and financial circumstances allow, you might take a more free-form sabbatical, by traveling or otherwise taking time off with less of a stated purpose in mind. While others might think you are vacationing, dropping out, or giving up, this break might be just what you need to gain some perspective and decide what to do next. (At one time this was referred to as a "year in Paris" or "round the world on a tramp steamer.")

Other possibilities include a stint with the Peace Corps or Ameri-Corps.

Starting Your Own Business

Virtually no one is likely to qualify (or survive) as an independent consultant until he or she has worked for at least a few years with an established consulting firm, nonprofit, or public agency, where there is much to be learned before striking out on one's own. Having completed your first few years' stint as an employee, you may now be feeling the call to become a freelance consultant, either working alone or in partnership with others. Among the possibilities are offering yourself as:

- A temporary employee to a short-staffed agency.

- A contractor to a government agency in search of an independent expert or assistance on a particular project (such as a general plan-making effort or some sort of project planning), and only for a fixed period of time.

- A specialist on a project-by-project basis on hire to another consultant whose staff does not include someone with your specialist skills (such as urban economics, urban design, fiscal analysis, environmental impact analysis, traffic studies, housing finance, report writing and editing).

- A specialist on hire to a real estate or housing developer as a creative project planner, lobbyist, or gun-for-hire in pursuit of a development permit, financing, or some other opportunity.

- A part-time or full-time advisor to a nonprofit in need of a particular skill at a particular time when there are no or only limited funds to hire permanent staff.

For any of these roles, there are no precise requisites other than having the skills that others are willing to pay for, plus a personality that is compatible with and suitable for work in the freelance arena, under circumstances that may be less than stable and probably not permanent. Of course, the more working experience you have, the better.

For some, setting up shop as a consultant may satisfy a need to be free of organizational frameworks and rules, at a time when perhaps the need to work alone (or to have time to raise children or deal with other responsibilities) is an overwhelming one. Others are driven by the perceived glamour and ego satisfaction associated with becoming an acknowledged expert, owning one's own business, or designing and occupying an office with one's name on the door ("The Sam Spade Complex").

More so even than in conventional employment settings, a consultant must have demonstrable and marketable skills. Business experience and instincts are also required; at the end of the day you must take in more revenue than you spend, and it is helpful to have some money left over to pay yourself a living wage or better.

The biggest mistakes made by people with a yen to strike out on their own are:

- Placing far too much importance on creating the dream office at a prestigious address, which can be a difficult-to-recover cost and an unnecessary expense at the beginning, as well as motivated too much by ego and too little by common sense. (Working at home in your den or on the dining room table, or in the garage as Bill Gates did, makes maximum good sense until you truly have abundant and stable income in hand.)

- Being under-capitalized, which means not having enough cash to set up even a rudimentary office with supplies and equipment plus a reserve to carry one over until contracts with clients produce revenue (perhaps as much as one year in the future). (This is called the "cash flow" dilemma.)

- Setting up shop too early in their professional careers—before they are credible in the eyes of potential clients and before they have enough paying work to keep themselves well above the water line.

- Failing to recognize that independent status, for all its very significant advantages and payoffs, remunerative and psychological, can have some huge disadvantages for many who try it: long hours (at least at the beginning), limited free time, the possibility of professional and social isolation, little separation between work life and personal life (especially if you work at home and/or cart around a lap top and a cell phone), and unpaid vacations that can usually be scheduled only at times convenient to the client.

Despite those potential pitfalls, you may find, as many have, that running your own business is a fun and rewarding way to spend your professional life.

WHAT TO DO WHILE YOU ARE "TREADING WATER"

Career planning, like other forms of planning, does not usually produce instant results.

Career planning, like the other forms of planning with which you are now familiar, does not usually produce instant results. Delays, uncertainties, and slow, small changes are much more typical. You may feel that you are treading water in your current job situation, while trying to sort yourself out and make changes happen. Here are a few steps you can take, and principles you can follow, that are bound to serve you well during this interim period (and even later, when you are happily ensconced in a new position).

- Keep your sense of humor and perspective. Much of what you may have to put up with may be absurd. Being earnest and a true believer may have got you into the field, but a sense of humor and perspective may do a lot to keep you there. Often workplace idiocy is temporary, so it will help to keep in mind: "This too shall pass."

- Talk with other people (colleagues, friends) about any feelings of angst or frustration you may be having. Others may have had similar experiences, and may offer useful suggestions for coping. You may find, too, that just talking helps ease the pain.

- Resist becoming a classic, rigid, and predictable bureaucrat. Please note the wording here. The problem is not in simply being a bureaucrat (which should not be regarded as a count against you if the public sector is the venue for the work you like to do), but in fitting the classic bureaucrat stereotype wherever it is that you work. It is prudent to keep a watchful eye on yourself to ward off tendencies to "act like a bureaucrat." Symptoms normally include losing enthusiasm, getting excessively caught up in office or agency procedures at the expense of the work being done, having a rather low energy level, and spending too much time at coffee breaks and lunch. If others around you are affected too, the workplace can become a languid culture that tends to feed on itself in nothing but negative ways.

Surviving in any bureaucracy, public or private, is a skill we learn on the job. Since survival skills are a form of self-preservation, most of us learn to survive while remaining effective, productive, and true to our own values. Others metamorphose into true bureaucrats without knowing, and even their friends won't tell them. You will know it is happening to you when the coffee break and covering up become more important than the real work you are asked to do. Growing with the flow means knowing how to work within the bureaucracy, or in spite of it, without adopting too many of its shortcomings. (And again, remember that bureaucracies prevail in the private sector as well as in the public.)

"One should treat an awkward job situation like a temporary love affair. Enjoy what you have embraced in the full knowledge that you'll be getting up to go on to better things soon."
—*A witty British friend*

- Focus your attention on developing your management, technology, and other skills. Learning about management makes sense even if you don't expect to become a top manager. You will be better able to manage yourself and your own work, and maybe even those who supervise you. Subjects most continuing education schools offer that can help you include: management principles, time management skills, how to cope with difficult people, oral presentations and public speaking, report writing, creative problem-solving techniques, executive effectiveness, working with employee associations or unions, organizational design and development, making the transition to a supervisory position, learning how to delegate authority and work, money management and budgeting, starting and running your own business, and new computer technologies.

All of the above can help you to maintain your integrity as a special person with unique attributes, capabilities, and skills. Try to build on the best of these. This will be important throughout your career, and essential to your survival during the treading water stage.

SOME FINAL THOUGHTS ON THE KEYS TO SUCCESS AND SURVIVAL

You may define success as achieving your own personal and career goals, satisfying your boss or client, causing a project to be accepted and adopted, coping during difficult times or episodes, and surviving in tough political situations. In most professional planning situations, survival and success come from following several guidelines.

First, don't expect a lot of appreciation. This is not to say it will not be expressed, but don't count on it all of the time. Focus on self-development so that you meet your needs first, followed by those of your boss or client.

Try not to become frustrated at the inevitable slow development of new ideas and programs. The democratic process moves along at its own pace. Learn to exercise patience, and stick to your guns; chances are you're going to be right, or at least helpful, much of the time.

Learn about and appreciate the passion, the occasional venom, and maybe even the deceitfulness and self-serving tactics of those who may oppose what you're doing or recommending. What you may think is a terrific idea or approach may be perceived by others as a threat to their power or financial security. And it's possible that not all of these people are truly wrongheaded or purely self-serving. Some may actually see the general welfare as their guiding principle.

In all situations with which you are associated as a practicing planner, be sure you are emotionally and intellectually equipped to apply standards of morality, fairness, and equity that will stand up to close scrutiny. Test yourself by following the cardinal rule: Above all else, ask who stands to benefit and who to lose by virtue of the recommendations, decisions, or actions you initiate. Can you do that in your current job, and throughout your career? A sense of success in the planning field comes from consistently applying this rule and using it as a guide in your professional actions.

Finally, remember that service on behalf of the public, which is what most of us do directly or indirectly, is a serious business— and a worthy one. If you are mindful of this and are continually finding ways of justifying your employment and your service to your client, you are more than likely going to be successful and content.

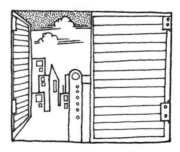

References and Bibliography

Books

Chan, Janis Fisher, and Diane Lutovich, *Professional Writing Skills: A Self-Paced Training Program*, Advanced Communication Designs, Inc., 2nd edition, 1997.

Cogan, Elaine, *Successful Public Meetings*, American Planning Association, 2000.

Hoch, Charles, *What Planners Do: Power, Politics*, and Persuasion, American Planning Association, 1994.

Macris, Natalie, *Planning in Plain English*, American Planning Association, 2000.

Zucker, Paul C., *The ABZs of Planning Management*, West Coast Publishers, 1997. *What Your Planning Professor Forgot to Tell You*, American Planning Association, 1999.

Videos

AICP Planners Training Service, "Writing Well," 1992.

American Planning Association Internet Resources

Resources for planners seeking employment (includes Internet links and a list of books available from APA Planners Book Service). See: *www.planning.org/switchbd/resource.html*

"Jobs Online." Help wanted ads for planners. See: *www.planning.org/jobs*

"The New Planner." A newsletter for APA student members. Offered only on the APA web site, not in print. See: *www.planning.org/abtapa/student.htm*

Information about the planning field. Answers these questions: What is planning? What do planners do? What skills does a planner need? See:
www.planning.org/educ/field.htm

"Seven Paths: Planners' Careers Move in Many Directions" (*Planning* magazine, December 1997). On the APA web site at *www.planning.org/PUBS/dec97.htm*

The Essential Planning Library Part II: Classic Articles from the *Journal of the American Planning Association*. Citations only, not full text. See:
www.planning.org/info/libpart2.htm

Chronological index of APA's Planning Advisory Service Reports (1949-1998). Citations only, not full text. See:
www.planning.org/pas/chron.html

Relevant items include:

— "Social Planning and City Planning." PAS Report 261. Michael P. Brooks. September 1970.

— "Planning, Women, and Change." PAS Report 301. Karen E. Hapgood and Judith N. Getzels. April 1974.

— "Job Descriptions for Planning Agencies." PAS Report 302. Daniel Lauber. May 1974.

— "Working With Consultants." PAS Report 378. Efraim Gil, Enid Lucchesi, Gilbert Tauber, and Dudley Onderdonk. September 1983.

— "Personnel Practices in Planning Offices." PAS Report 434. Carolyn M.R. Kennedy. August 1991.

— "Planners' Salaries and Employment Trends." PAS Report 464. Marya Morris. July 1996.

Authors' Note

The following parts of this book are adapted from its predecessor, *What Do I Do Next? A Manual For People Just Entering Government Service* by Warren W. Jones and Albert Solnit (American Planning Association, 1980).

Chapter 1: The Planning Profession and You
"Finding the Right Environment For You"—adapted from *What Do I Do Next?*, pages x-xi.

Chapter 2: What Employers Are Looking For
"Essential Skills Required"—adapted from *What Do I Do Next?*, pages 27-31.

Chapter 3: Landing Your First Job
"The Job Market: Myths and Realities"—adapted from *What Do I Do Next?*, page 95 (based in part on Julie Monson, "In the Meantime: A Strategy for Job Hunters," Pomona Today (Pomona College alumni magazine), March 1975, page 7).

"Weighing Your Chances"—adapted from *What Do I Do Next?*, page 89.

"Filling Out Applications"—portions adapted from *What Do I Do Next?*, pages 89-90.

"Writing Resumes"—portions adapted from *What Do I Do Next?*, page 91.

"Writing Cover Letters"—portions adapted from *What Do I Do Next?*, pages 91-92.

"Before the Interview"—adapted from *What Do I Do Next?*, pages 98-99.

"Preparing for the Interview"—adapted from *What Do I Do Next?*, pages 99-100.

"A Few More Questions to Expect"—adapted from *What Do I Do Next?*, pages 96 and 98.

"During the Interview"—adapted from *What Do I Do Next?*, pages 98-99.

"Overwhelmed? Here's Your Basic Homework"—adapted from *What Do I Do Next?*, pages 102- 103.

Chapter 4: What To Expect From Your Job
"Your Workplace: Insiders and Outsiders"—portions adapted from *What Do I Do Next?*, pages 7-21.

Chapter 6: Essential Communication Skills
"Giving and Following Directions"—adapted from *What Do I Do Next?*, pages 31-32.

"Communicating Upward"—adapted from *What Do I Do Next?*, pages 32-33.

"Communicating With the Public"—adapted from *What Do I Do Next?*, pages 33-34.

"Presenting Yourself in Public"—adapted from *What Do I Do Next?*, pages 35-36.

Chapter 7: Essential Management Skills
"Making Decisions"—portions adapted from *What Do I Do Next?*, pages 62-63.

"Developing Work Programs"—adapted from *What Do I Do Next?*, pages 50-53.

"Being a Project Manager"—portions adapted from *What Do I Do Next?*, pages 53-56.

"Handling Foul-Ups"—adapted from *What Do I Do Next?*, page 57.

"Managing Time Spent in Meetings"—portions adapted from *What Do I Do Next?*, page 56.

"Managing Paperwork"—portions adapted from *What Do I Do Next?*, pages 64-66.

Chapter 10: Setting a Career Path for Yourself
Introduction—adapted from *What Do I Do Next?*, pages 77-78.

"Is It Time to Move On?"—portions adapted from *What Do I Do Next?*, pages 112-113.

About the Authors

Warren W. Jones

In the 1950s, after receiving an undergraduate degree in political science and linguistics (Chinese), I found the idea of city planning, then still in its infancy, intriguing enough to seek and earn a master's degree in city planning at the University of California at Berkeley. After working for about five years in local government, the switch to a professional life as a freelance consultant seemed to be a logical progression and my rightful calling. (I remain in that role, albeit now on a strictly pro-bono basis in the role of chairman of my small town's general plan preparation citizens advisory committee.) In 1972, the University of California appointed me director of continuing professional education in planning and environmental design. I held that post for 15 years while also teaching part-time in Berkeley's graduate city and regional planning program. In 1985, I established a small book publishing company that today produces books, reference guides, and manuals for planning professionals, attorneys, college students, and public officials on planning and environmental law and practice.

When I was a graduate student in the 1950s, planning as a function of government was in its formative years. Those were somewhat heady times, when there were just a few of us and all of us believed that we were destined to save our cities and landscapes through the application of planning principles. Since then the profession has grown up and broadened its scope, and planners have expanded their roles dramatically while also shedding their earlier naivete. Along the way we defined our unique roles in a variety of settings while also learning that there are many other legitimate actors in the dramas of which we are a part: activist citizens, politicians, other professionals, for-profit special interests of all kinds, nonprofit single-purpose special interests, and others. We work in the public sector at all levels of government and for all sorts of nonpublic enterprises. We are engaged in planning activities not even imagined in the mid-1950s. Most of us who started out in the 1950s and witnessed planning's gradual maturity have had rich and satisfying careers as public agency planners, and others metamorphosed into consultants, professors, citizen activists, chief executives, and even political figures. I've passed through all of those incarnations. It has been a challenging, sometimes dramatic, and occasionally daunting journey.

While teaching at Berkeley I developed the somewhat (for the time) revolutionary notion that once college-educated novitiate planners hit the streets they entered an unknown and highly politicized world that was barely acknowledged within academia—and they were often not as well prepared to do so as their new employers had hoped. As a consequence, the ideas that form the basis for this book were born at Berkeley, tested over many years, and now appear here in print. I hope the book will benefit those who enter the "real world" of planning, however you define it and in whatever venues present themselves, in the 21st century.

Warren Jones   *Natalie Macris*

Natalie Macris

I have worked as an urban and environmental planner since 1985, when I received a masters degree in city planning from the University of California at Berkeley. After two years as a planner for a small city in northern California, I moved to the private sector, working for consulting offices where I conducted environmental reviews and helped prepare plans. At the five-year point in my career, I took a break and spent 10 months traveling around the world and doing volunteer work for an environmental education group. Since 1991, I have been self-employed as a planner, writer, and editor, working with planning consultants, architects, public agencies, and nonprofit organizations.

In a sense, my planning education began long before graduate school. In the time and place where I grew up (California in the 1970s), environmental concerns were gaining recognition and were being discussed even in grade schools. In college, I majored in American history and studied cultural attitudes toward cities and the history of the built environment. And since both of my parents are city planners, the planning field was in some ways already familiar to me when I started graduate school. My interest in environmental issues and cultural history, as well as the idea of carrying on a "family business," are what led me to a career in planning.

In thinking about my parents' careers, and then later my own, two questions have always interested me. One is how the more obvious disadvantages of working in the planning field (long hours, acrimonious public meetings, inevitable compromises, and usually respectable but less-than-glamorous pay) are offset by the important, but often less tangible rewards (intellectual stimulation, and a sense of contributing to a greater good). The other is how to match each person's particular skills and talents to the right job in a field as broad as ours is.

The predecessor to this book, *What Do I Do Next?*, has been useful to me in considering these questions. I hope you will find this new book a valuable and entertaining guide for finding your way in the planning world.

Index

Co-workers, tips for dealing with, 5860
Credentials, 3334

D
Deadlines, missing, 14445
Decision making, 9799
Democracy in America, 119
Department administrators, tips for dealing with, 6163
Department head, tips for dealing with, 61
Departments, tips for dealing with people from other, 6364
Direct approach as source of job opening, 37
Direct citizen actions, 12223
Directions, giving and following, 8990
Directors
    attributes of, 99100
    tips for dealing with, 61
Discouragement, handling, 147
Dislikes, 155

E
Education, continuing, 158
Elected officials, tips for dealing with, 6869
E-mail, using, 11617
Employers
    culture at, 7174
    skills sought by, 2332
Employment interview. See Job Interview
Employment services as source of job opening, 36
Ethical issues, 8083
Experts, belief in, 14142

F
Foul-ups, handling, 112

G
Generalist skills, 26
GIS mapping, 5
Graphics, 9394
Group maintenance roles for co-workers, 5859

H
Headhunter, seeking out, 158
Help, asking for, 14445

I
Immediate supervisor, tips for dealing with, 60
Individual citizens, tips for dealing with, 6566
Informational interviews, 158
Intentions, surviving on good, 146
Internet listings as source of job opening, 3536
Interview. See Job Interview

J
Job interview
    actions following, 50
    basic homework for, 5051
    handling yourself during, 4849

O